THE UNIVERSAL BROTHER

Charles de Foucauld Speaks to Us Today

Published by New City Press
202 Comforter Blvd.,
Hyde Park, NY 12538
www.newcitypress.com

©2019 New City Press

Cover design and layout: Miguel Tejerina
Photos and drawings: *Little Sisters of Jesus*

The Universal Brother:
Charles de Foucauld Speaks to Us Today
Library of Congress Control Number: 2018967123

ISBN 978-1-56548-646-1 (paperback)
ISBN 978-1-56548-647-8 (e-book)

Printed in the United States of America

THE UNIVERSAL BROTHER

Charles de Foucauld Speaks to Us Today

Little Sister Kathleen of Jesus

New City Press
Hyde Park, New York

Charles de Foucauld, a modern-day desert father, invented a new style of contemplative life, inspired by the hidden life that Jesus spent as a carpenter in Nazareth. Foucauld attracted no followers in his life, which ended in 1918 in a remote corner of Algeria. Today, however, his influence extends far beyond the communities inspired by his witness. Truly, he was one of the great saints of modern times. In this beautiful and intimate account of his life and spiritual message, one of his followers, Little Sister Kathleen brings his story to life and shows how keenly his message speaks to our age.

Robert Ellsberg
Editor, *Charles de Foucauld: Writings*

Even those who are familiar with the life of Charles de Foucauld will find many new insights in Little Sister Kathleen's book. It's more than a biography: it's a guide for all of us to living the life of Nazareth; the life of "everyday holiness" as Pope Francis calls it. The Brother Charles who emerges from these pages is alive, endearing, and inspiring.

Rev. Terrence J. Moran
Office of Peace, Justice and Ecological Integrity,
Sisters of Charity of Saint Elizabeth

Little Sister Kathleen's biography of Charles de Foucauld is very special. One not only learns details about de Foucauld's life that one had not known before, but Sister Kathleen provides many personal insights into the implications of de Foucuald's spirituality for today. In a world where Islam is so important and where poverty of all types abounds, he calls us to a universal openness. He calls us - whatever one's walk of life - to a spirituality of abandonment into God's hands, encounter with others and the fostering of community, especially with the poor. In a word, he is our universal brother. I highly recommend this book.

Msgr. Richard M. Liddy
Seton Hall University

Contents

Map of the region Charles de Foucauld lived in

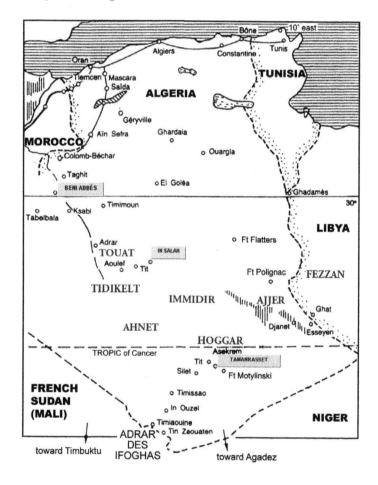

1

A Short Biography

As night fell on December 1, 1916, Charles de Foucauld died alone in Tamanrasset, a tiny *arrem*[1] in the Algerian Sahara where he had built his hermitage eleven years earlier. Far from any European capitals and the events making headlines during the Great War, his death went largely unnoticed. Yet his embodiment of God's scandalous choice to become man at Nazareth was to make him one of the most influential figures of the Church in the twentieth century. "To be rich and secure, living leisurely off my wealth, when you were poor, needy, and toiled for your living . . . as for me, I couldn't do it, my God. I couldn't love like that."[2] His spiritual adventure, lived in the midst of a Muslim population, recalls the extent to which God has established the margins as his meeting place with humanity.

His spiritual quest, which today inspires some twenty-one congregations (among them the Little Sisters of Jesus, to which I belong) led him through many twists and turns along a road that stretched from Strasbourg to the far-flung reaches of the Sahara.

---

1. Group of huts and gardens forming a village.
2. Meditation, Nazareth, November 11, 1897. Editor's note: Translations of de Foucauld's writings and correspondence are done by the author.

Bittersweet memories

Son of an aristocratic French family, Charles de Foucauld was born in 1858, a time when social class mattered a great deal.

He would later speak of bittersweet childhood memories: sweet because he was a well-loved child, bitter because he lost both parents at a very young age. When Charles was four, his father began to show signs of mental illness and was sent to an asylum. The blow affected his young wife so deeply that she died one year later. Both Charles and his younger sister Marie (Mimi) were raised by their grandfather in Strasbourg. Holidays were spent in their Aunt Ines's château. She had two daughters, the youngest of whom, Marie, would have a decisive influence on his life.

After the Franco-Prussian war in 1870, Alsace was annexed by Germany. Charles's grandfather opted to leave Strasbourg and settle in Nancy.

Of a solitary nature, Charles had a friend, Gabriel Tourdes, with whom he shared a passion for literature. At fifteen he ceased to believe in God, something he later attributed to the way he and Gabriel "devoured books."[3] After three years of secondary education in Nancy, his grandfather decided to send him to a Jesuit-run school in Paris, hoping it would open the way to a prestigious institute of higher learning. Unfortunately, it only ended with his expulsion, "laziness being not the only reason."[4] His decision to embark on a military career resulted more from poor marks than an active interest in the military. He spent two years at Saint-Cyr, an academy that trained officers.

---

3. Letter to Gabriel Tourdes, March 27, 1877.
4. Letter to Marie de Bondy, April 19, 1892.

When Charles was twenty years old, the death of his grandfather, whose "infinite tenderness" enveloped his youth, brought "immense sorrow."[5] From Saint-Cyr he moved on to cavalry school at Saumur. The curriculum held no interest for him, and despite his brilliant mind, he came out eighty-seventh of eighty-seven students. His family became increasingly concerned about the lavish loans he extended to his friends.

At the age of twenty-two he was sent as a sub-lieutenant to a garrison on the German border where he became involved with a young woman. Was it a meaningful relationship or did he simply use her as a means of getting out of a dreary job? His refusal to send her away resulted in his suspension from the army, leading one biographer to theorize that the involvement had then achieved its purpose, and Charles felt no real attachment to the woman.[6] Whatever his feelings might have been, he had "hardly begun to taste the pleasures of life in a lakeside resort in Switzerland" when a letter from a comrade informed him that part of their regiment was involved in combat in Tunisia. Stating that this was "too rare a pleasure not to try to take part,"[7] Charles requested that his suspension be revoked, promising that he would have nothing further to do with his mistress. The army did indeed take him back, but sent him to Algeria where France was pursuing a vast colonial offensive. Charles took part in operations against Marabutic tribes in the High Plateaus on the Moroccan border. He wrote to Gabriel, "Camp life pleases me as much as life in a garrison displeases me, and that's really saying something."[8] Once the fighting was over he asked

---

5. Letter to Henri Duveyrier, February 21, 1892.
6. See Pierre Sourisseau, *Charles de Foucauld (1858-1916): Biographie*, Paris: Salvator, 2016.
7. Both quotes, Letter to Gabriel Tourdes, October 2, 1881.
8. Ibid.

to be sent elsewhere where there was action. His request was denied, so he decided to quit the army and go travelling. His renewed impulsive behavior led his family to place him under the watch of a legal guardian.

Pathway to conversion

His desire to travel turned into plans for a daring exploration of Morocco. Europeans were barred from the inland areas, and fighting among the tribes made the journey a most perilous enterprise. He spent the better part of fifteen months at the library of Algiers preparing, learning Arabic and acquiring cartographic skills. Barred from travelling as a European and insufficiently fluent in Arabic, he chose to pass himself off as a Jew, hiring a Moroccan Jew named Mardochee to act as guide. The two set off in June 1883 and spent almost a year exploring the country. Charles had several close brushes with death but was always rescued in the name of sacred hospitality. From his expedition, his encounter with Islam and experience of poverty and hospitality would leave their lasting mark on him.

Back in Algiers Charles set about publishing his findings, and in April 1885, the Paris Geographical Society granted him its gold medal.

Just at the moment when a brilliant career was opening up, deeper questions began to surface in Charles's inner life. He probed the writings of philosophers and moralists but found no light. In February 1886, he decided to settle in Paris, tightening bonds with his family, especially with his cousin Marie, now Madame de Bondy. Her faith-inspired life touched him and he confided his inner search to her. She pointed him in the direction of Fr. Huvelin. Even though he was only the curate in the neighborhood parish, St. Augustine, he was a well-known figure in Paris and his conferences attracted a wide audience. Charles had decided to take part in a series planned for November 1886, but it had to be cancelled due to Fr. Huvelin's bad health. Toward the end of October that year, he resolved to ask Fr. Huvelin for private religion lessons. Rather than comply with his request, the latter invited him to the confessional. Charles's conversion was radical. He was twenty-eight years old.

The tale of his trip to Morocco was published in February 1888, but already Charles's energies were turned elsewhere. He met with Fr. Huvelin for spiritual direction almost daily. Given Charles's past as an explorer, Fr. Huvelin suggested a pilgrimage to the Holy Land. Charles spent two months there, and walking the streets of Nazareth turned out to be an overwhelming experience. He returned with the conviction that his vocation was to follow in the footsteps of the One who "took the last place."

What would that mean concretely? On a visit to a Trappist abbey with his cousin, he was struck by the patched-up habit worn by the porter. Here at last was a community that "lived Nazareth." Fr. Huvelin made some inquiries and learned that a Trappist monastery in central France had just founded a priory in Akbes, Syria.[9] Given Charles's attraction to Arab countries, Fr. Huvelin pointed him in their direction.

Seven years as a Trappist

Charles was thirty-one when he entered the monastery of Our Lady of the Snows in France. A few months later he was sent to Akbes. The monks were greatly impressed by the asceticism of their new postulant who had relin-

---

9.   The monastery of Our Lady of the Snows feared expropriation by the new republican French government and wanted to prepare a refuge.

quished fortune and career. But Charles would always claim that his one and only sacrifice was leaving his family.[10] This doesn't mean he broke the connection, because he would always have ample correspondence with his family, especially with his cousin Marie. The two of them made a mutual promise to always tell "the whole truth."

Along with the habit, Charles received the name of Brother Marie Alberic. The abbot, Dom Martin, said of him, "I have never met anyone who emanated such holiness."[11] The novice master was more reserved, expressing concern over a "perfection that's too great to last."[12] In fact Charles only lasted seven years. He had chosen the Trappists because their way of life seemed to correspond to his vision of Nazareth. But problems appeared as soon as he perceived a gap between his ideal and the reality of life in a monastery, even a very poor one. Troubled, Charles decided to refer the discernment of his vocation to the Abbot General. The latter invited him to Rome, and did not take long to conclude that Charles was called elsewhere. Charles left the Trappists in January 1897, but his monastic formation would always accompany him.

From the hermitage to a fraternity

Somewhat perplexed, Fr. Huvelin again took up his role as spiritual director. Charles asked to return to the Holy Land in order to live the life of the "divine workman of Nazareth." Arriving at the Poor Clare monastery in Nazareth, he inquired if they were in need of a workman.

---

10. Antoine Chatelard, *Bulletin des Amitiés Charles de Foucauld*, July 1990, no. 97, p. 8.
11. Dom Martin to Msgr. Guerin, February 11, 1902.
12. Dom Polycarpe to his sister, Mother Clemence of Jesus, March 19, 1891.

Aware of his true identity, the sisters offered him a room, but he spotted a tool shed behind their wall. It was to become his hermitage for three years. His services to the sisters consisted mostly in serving at Mass and going to the post office.

These years brought moments of great illumination but also of intense dryness. Fr. Huvelin advised him to put his meditations into writing in order to help clarify his thinking. In a desire to be the little brother of the One whom he called the "Only Model," he pored over the gospel, saturating his mind and soul with Jesus' words. He would later say that no passage in the gospel transformed his life more deeply than Matthew's account of the final judgement: "Truly, I say to you, as you did it to one of the least of these my brethren, you did it to me."[13] These words, which reveal Jesus' presence in the "least," would end up pushing him out of the hermitage into a fraternity.

The Mother Abbess of the Poor Clares in Jerusalem was keen to meet the venerable servant-hermit of her sisters in Nazareth, so the sisters found an excuse to send him to Jerusalem. Under her influence, Charles began to think of the priesthood, something he had always rejected as contrary to his calling to "go down." Dismayed that no one had joined Jesus in leading his life of Nazareth, Charles dreamed of founding a congregation he wished to call the *Hermits of the Sacred Heart*. The foundation of such an order, however, would require him to be a priest. He returned to Paris to consult with his spiritual director. Perplexed with all these changes of orientation, Fr. Huvelin nevertheless directed Charles toward the altar. The Trappists at Our Lady of the Snows agreed to prepare him for priesthood and he was eventually ordained by the bishop of Viviers.

---

13. Matthew 25:40. See verses 31-46 for the entire passage.

Retreats preceding his ordination were moments of great insight regarding his special vocation. His gospel meditations led him to understand that the divine banquet must be offered not to friends and family but, as he often noted, to the "most lame, those seated in the deepest shadow." The faces of the people he met during his expedition to Morocco now came back to mind. He was called not to be a hermit but a brother.

The universal brother

Since Morocco was still closed to Europeans, Charles began to think of settling on the Algerian side of the border. In spite of the tension that dominated relations between Church and state, in very little time he received all the necessary military and ecclesiastical permissions. A new apostolic prefecture had just been created in the Sahara with a young White Father, Msgr. Guérin, at its head. He welcomed Charles to Algiers on September 10, 1901. By October the newcomer was already settled in Beni Abbès, a big oasis in the Algerian Saoura, a region that had only recently been occupied by French forces.

Marie de Bondy's financial generosity allowed Charles to buy land halfway between the walled villages of the local population and the French garrison. The army supplied workmen who built him a little monastery that he called the *Fraternity of the Sacred Heart of Jesus*. He immediately planted a palm grove that could feed from twenty-five to thirty little brothers. He marked the boundaries of his cloister with a line of big stones. He himself would rarely go beyond it, but anyone could enter. He wished to be a universal brother in a context of conflict involving many opposing parties. The poor, slaves, and soldiers flooded in, with him all alone to assume the duties of a fraternity built for twenty-five little brothers! The latter, in fact, were the only ones who did not come. Even though he had everyone's admiration, there were hesitations about sending him candidates. Who could keep up with him?

Among the Tuareg people

In June 1903, the newly-named commander of the Saharan Oases, General Laperrine, asked Charles to take part in "pacification tours" he was organizing among the Tuareg nomads of the Sahara. Occupation of the Sahara required their submission and Laperrine preferred a peaceful entente to one made at gunpoint. He knew the influence a holy man might have on them. Laperrine tried to gain Charles's interest by telling him the story of Tarichat oult Ibdakane, a Tuareg woman who had intervened during a skirmish to save the lives of a few soldiers of the French army. Charles was greatly impressed at the natural virtue of someone who had manifested such love of the enemy, but still he hesitated to go. He was forty-five years old by this time, and the journey implied trekking thousands of miles in extreme conditions and in the company of soldiers. He had only just settled in Beni Abbès. Laperrine's invitation disturbed him, yet also corresponded to a desire he carried within: to bring Jesus to those who were furthest away. No priest had ever been among the Tuareg before. He saw himself going to them like Mary in the mystery of the Visitation, carrying Jesus to her cousin Elizabeth. At the same time, he knew that it was the poor who revealed Jesus to him. The journey toward the abandoned people of the Sahara would lead him to a new form of contemplation, based not on leaving the world, but on human relationships.

As he set out on these pacification tours that would extend over three years, he felt the ambiguity of his presence among the military. General Laperrine was also aware of it, writing to the captain of the garrison at Beni Abbès: "If

I see that he gets on well with the Tuareg, I'll set him loose. My dream is to make him the first vicar of the Hoggar,[14] Moussa's chaplain. I prefer to see him far from us. Let people get used to seeing him without bayonets all around."[15]

A spiritual and anthropological undertaking

Right from the very beginning Charles thought of settling among the Tuareg, but they were nomads, and in order to meet them he too had to move. The first year he covered almost six thousand kilometers, most of them on foot. On his return to Beni Abbès in January 1905, he was exhausted and anxious to return to a life lived according to his rule. But he had hardly arrived back when he received an invitation to set out on yet another tour. He thought of refusing, but both Fr. Huvelin and Msgr. Guérin encouraged him to accept. No other priest was allowed a mission among the Tuareg and he was being invited. During this second tour, he met the Tuareg chief of the Hoggar, Moussa ag Amastane, who had missed his meeting with the French military the previous year. He gave Charles permission to settle in Tamanrasset. Made up of twenty campfires, the village seemed so isolated and forgotten that Charles chose it as that "last place" so suited to his vocation. In six days he built his hermitage of stone and mud, after which the military convoy left him with a promise to try to establish a monthly postal run. Charles wrote to his cousin, "I will remain alone, happy, very happy to be alone with Jesus, alone for Jesus."[16]

---

14. Mountainous region in the central Sahara, stronghold of the Kel Ahaggar (people of the Hoggar) whose amenokal (chief) at the time was Moussa ag Amastan.
15. General Laperrine to Captain Regnault, February 19, 1904.
16. Letter to Marie de Bondy, August 26, 1905.

The beginnings were in fact far from easy. The Tuareg nomads roamed in search of pasture while the villagers, mostly Harratins, cultivated gardens in places where underground water ran close to the surface. All were wary of this stranger who had been brought by the occupying army, resenting the fact that they needed to share their meager water resources with him.

Brother Charles immediately set about studying the Tuareg language, known as *Tamahaq* in southern Algeria. He solicited help from a friend in Algiers, Adolphe Motylinski, who came to Tamanrasset for three months. Charles hoped that Motylinski, an expert in Berber languages, would undertake a systematic study of Tamahaq, while he himself would compile a simple lexicon that could be of use to future missionaries. But Motylinski died only a few months after his return to Algiers, leaving the project to Charles.

Some modern linguists regret that Charles de Foucauld's spiritual personality has eclipsed the scientific value of his undertaking. But for him, spirituality and knowledge of the Tuareg people were not separable. "I can do good to the Tuareg only by knowing their language well and speaking with them."[17] His neighbors were impressed by his attention, confessing, "He knows our language better than we do ourselves."[18]

The apostolate of friendship

Having set off for the Hoggar in the hope that people like Tarichat oult Ibdakane would be open to the gospel, brother Charles[19] slowly realized that his vocation was not

17. Letter to Fr. Huvelin, December 4, 1909.
18. Bazin, p. 290.
19. Charles wrote "brother" this way with his name to empha-

to convert others but to prepare the terrain through culti-
vating a reciprocal attitude of goodwill.

> My apostolate should be one of goodness. When
> people see me they should say, "If this man is good,
> his religion must be good." If someone asks me
> why I am gentle and good, I should say: "Because
> I am the servant of someone much better than I
> am. If you only knew how good my master Jesus
> is." I want to be good enough that people will say:
> "If this is what the servant is like, what must the
> master be?"[20]

In 1910 he asked masons building Fort Motylinski,
fifty kilometers from Tamanrasset, to build him a second
hermitage on Assekrem, in a magnificent setting among
the Hoggar Mountains. Surrounded by rich pastures, he
hoped he would meet more Tuareg there. "Spending one
day or even half a day together binds you to each other
more closely than any number of half-hour or one-hour
visits as in Tamanrasset."[21] He spent six months in Assekrem. But the tough climate and extremely poor diet
gradually proved detrimental to his health.

On his return to Tamanrasset in December 1911 he
was saddened to witness the growing poverty. It was to
him that the local people would address their complaints
about the French administration's misuse of power. He
grieved to see France enriching itself from its colonies
without committing itself to improving the situation of
people who were already so destitute. He began to nurse
the idea of founding an association that would awaken
Christians back in the homeland to their duties. He trav-

---

size his desire for littleness.
20. Notes summarizing advice given by Fr. Huvelin in 1909.
21. Letter to Marie de Bondy, August 15, 1911.

eled to France three times in the hope of starting what he named the *Union of the Brothers and Sisters of the Sacred Heart*. He toiled at drawing up statutes. And in spite of his old-fashioned style of writing, some people, such as renowned scholar of Islam Louis Massignon, perceived how important and relevant his project might be.

The last day

The Great War which broke out in 1914 put his plans to start a Union on the back burner. France's military efforts, which until then had been aimed at Algeria, had now to be redirected to the front in Europe, leaving the Sahara much more vulnerable. Moroccan raiders took advantage of the situation and their incursions became more frequent, drawing ever nearer to the Hoggar. Cultivators of the land, such as the local population in Tamanrasset, were a permanent temptation for these raiders. Having spoken with his neighbours, Charles decided to build a *bordj*, a little fort where people could store their grain and seek refuge in case of attack. Brickmaking began in June 1915, and by August walls one meter thick and twenty meters long (about three feet thick and sixty-five feet long) began to emerge out of the sand.

But while the residents of Tamanrasset had their attention fixed on Morocco, the real threat was gathering momentum in the east. Several Tuareg tribes had already been won over to the cause of the Senussi, a Muslim confraternity that preached jihad against the European invaders. When the Senussi drove the Italian occupying forces out of the south of Tripolitania, they came into possession of the large quantity of arms, including three cannons which the Italians had left behind. The threat to Tamanrasset increased dramatically. At the request of the local residents, Charles took up residence in the *bordj*.

The French army stocked it with guns so that the people would be able to defend themselves in case of an attack.

As evening fell on the first of December 1916, an armed grouped of Senussi silently made their way up the wadi to Tamanrasset. The postman had passed by earlier on his way to Fort Motylinski, and brother Charles had spent his day writing letters that would be picked up on the postman's return trip that evening or the following morning. Pretending to be the expected postman, one of the attackers managed to get Charles to open the door. Charles was bound hand and foot and left under the guard of a sixteen-year-old while the group ransacked the little fort. Did they intend to take him as a hostage? Question him later? Twenty minutes later several unsuspecting Arab soldiers, who served in the French army and who had just arrived in Tamanrasset, came to the fort to greet the *marabout*.[22] Gunfire broke out as they drew near. Charles's young guard panicked, put his gun to his head and shot him. At fifty-eight, Charles's life was over.

The next morning villagers buried his body along with that of the three Muslims killed during the attack. Charles was not to appear before the face of God without his "brothers."

A new approach to mission

Saddened by his tragic end, the White Fathers and later Louis Massignon asked the renowned French author René Bazin to write Charles's story. Published in 1923, it made a public hero of him and in 1927 the cause for his beatification was opened (he was beatified in 2005). In spite of his written wish to be buried where he died, his body was moved to El Goléa in 1929 for public veneration. The

---

22. A holy man.

inscription on his grave reads: "I want to cry the Gospel with my whole life." These words summarized his new approach to mission, which relied more on what one *was* rather than what one said.

Numerous men and women have followed in his footsteps. Today many congregations, as well as numerous lay and priestly associations, claim his spiritual legacy. The Little Sisters of Jesus, my community, were founded by little sister Magdeleine in 1939. Rather than weakening with time, an interest in Charles de Foucauld continues to grow in a world where love of humankind doesn't always coincide with love of God and where dialogue easily deteriorates into confrontation.

The uniqueness of brother Charles doesn't reside so much in his ideas as in the radicalness with which he put into practice what he understood of the gospel. All of his journey can be summed up in three words that often appear in his writing: "When one loves . . ."

2

My Discovery of a Friend

I was seventeen years old when I encountered brother Charles for the first time. I must admit that our first meeting didn't go so well. I was just back from nine months in Mexico on a student exchange. Things had started out well but ended rather badly. The program director had even accompanied me to the airport to make sure I went back! In Toronto, my parents were waiting for me. There wasn't a single question; they were just happy to have me back safe and sound. Without realizing it at the time, I had just undergone the experience of the prodigal daughter.

The school year hadn't yet begun and I had a lot of time on my hands. In our house, there were shelves of books and one title drew my attention: *Letters from the Desert* by a certain Carlo Carretto. I started reading. The author narrated his life as a novice with the Little Brothers of Jesus in the Sahara. His description of the night sky in the desert mesmerized me. The stars not only sang the Creator's power but their beauty also hinted that love was at the origin of all this. And the Creator seemed to be inviting us to take part in his life by becoming loving ourselves.

Carlo Carretto wrote that the little brothers and sisters didn't live just in the Sahara but in the deserts of the modern world: factories, big cities, slums. In choosing Nazareth, God had made the life of little people a place of revelation. I am not aware of having searched for my vocation: it came to meet me. In reading Carretto's book I seemed to discover my own hidden desires. It was so strange and yet so much in keeping with the gospel that my vocation came to meet me at a time when I had lost my bearings. I could almost say that I didn't give much consideration to the fact that entering the Little Sisters meant embarking on religious life. The attraction of a contemplative life "in the marketplace" began to shine for me like the star of Bethlehem, indicating a journey. And in spite of many nights, that little light has never gone out.

The only thing that bored me in the book were lengthy passages dedicated to a former French soldier, Charles de Foucauld, who had converted in the nineteenth century and gone to live in the Sahara. I didn't understand why Carretto spoke about him so much.

Later on, I searched for other books on the little brothers and little sisters. I went to the university library but found nothing. There were only a few books about Charles de Foucauld, whom I finally understood to be the founder . . . but those volumes were so old and dusty that I left them on the shelves.

Years passed but the attraction did not. Quite the contrary. And on the eve of my twenty-fourth birthday I joined the Little Sisters of Jesus in Montreal. After years at university that had bored me, I was delighted to embark on a way of life that had attracted me for so long. I quickly found a job in a fast food joint and my life of prayer began to bear the stamp of the working world in which I was immersed. It's what the founder of the Little Brothers of Jesus, Father Voillaume, calls "The Prayer of Poor People." I still remember the window through which noise from the neighborhood used to pour into the chapel. Far from distracting me, it grounded me in conditions similar to what life must have been like in Nazareth, where Jesus, Mary, and Joseph led their life of contemplation for thirty years.

My second meeting with the one whom I now call *brother* Charles happened during my postulancy. The oldest little sister in the region, Réjeanne, had been asked to speak to me about him. She was an eighty-year-old Québécoise who really had her feet on the ground. She didn't theorize about him too much. In fact, the only thing I recall from her talk was that while she was in the Sahara she had nearly drowned while crossing a wadi that was in full spate. She cried out, "Fr. de Foucauld, save me!" and she survived. Her little story was a striking contrast to all the spiritual writings of brother Charles that filled the shelves. They seemed so ethereal that I wondered how little sister Réjeanne had ever had the idea of calling on him in such a perilous moment.

Within the Montreal community, one of the little sisters was experiencing doubts about her vocation. She felt attracted by the Carmelite order and so it was decided that she would spend a few months there in order to make a clearer discernment. When she returned I asked her how she had found it. She complimented the Carmelites, saying, "They have such a strong sense of their founders." That challenged me. What did my founders mean in my own life? In spite of my best efforts I just couldn't feel any affinity with brother Charles. I loved the writings of Fr. Voillaume and little sister Magdeleine. They opened up vast horizons for me. But brother Charles remained a closed book.

In 1990 I joined the group of twenty-eight little sisters who were preparing for final vows in our motherhouse in Aix-en-Provence. I stopped in Paris on the way to visit my grandmother. St. Augustine Church is there, where brother Charles experienced his big conversion. Even if I was on the verge of making final vows I still had a lot of questions about the community and myself. Among other things, chastity continued to be a thorn in my flesh; it had been since the beginning. I choked up when I saw brother Charles's confessional and the little sign hanging on the door, which read, "In October 1886 Charles de Foucauld was converted here." The church was empty and so I sat a long while on the step where he had knelt to confide all my struggles to him. I felt at ease with him because he was no stranger to these kinds of difficulties. A relationship began that day.

During that year of preparation for final vows we had a session with a little brother who seemed to feel a call to demythologize Charles de Foucauld. He went about it with great gusto, knocking the gold out of any halo our imaginations may have wreathed about his head. It wasn't the most helpful approach for me who already had trouble with him. I couldn't keep the difference straight between Beni Abbès or Tamanrasset and to my mind an Arab, a Tuareg, or a Kabyle were all the same thing. It was only many years later that I could appreciate what that brother was about, making brother Charles more human and speaking about him with a language that was more up to date.

The date chosen for my final vows was December 1, the anniversary of brother Charles's death. I was surrounded by friends and family on the day that I said yes forever. I said it with great trust. Just before my vows I had experienced a friendship with a man which could have become more than just a friendship. In deciding to make my vows instead of pursuing this relationship, I experienced just how deeply God wanted me to be free and empowered to make a real choice. I chose to continue in the steps of brother Charles, seeking that *greater* love.

For the ceremony itself I chose as the first reading a passage from a letter brother Charles wrote to his cousin on the day of his death:

> When we can suffer and love we can do much. We can do the most that can be done in this world. We can feel that we are suffering; we cannot always feel that we are loving, and that adds another great suffering! But we know we want to love, and to want to love is to love. We feel that we don't love sufficiently; how true. We will never love enough, but God, who does

not lie, who knows the clay from which he fashioned us and who loves us more than a mother can love her child, said that he would not refuse the one who came to him.[23]

In spite of a few luminous passages, Charles de Foucauld's meditations remained largely inaccessible, saturated with a sentimentality that turned me off. It was Fr. Voillaume who would provide me with the key. I had grabbed one of his booklets as I went off to the hermitage for two days of prayer. It was a session he had given for the little sisters in Rome. In it, he said that you needed to learn to read brother Charles's meditations, paying attention not so much to what he wrote as to the huge amount of work he had done to get to know Jesus, because, "You cannot love what you do not know." In one instant his words cast an entirely new light on those pages, and other pages of brother Charles's writings. I no longer saw them as tiresome repetitive meditations, but an effort of love. How resolutely he had worked to get to know Jesus! Often we read the Word of God superficially and use it to shore up our own ideas. Brother Charles, to the contrary, had searched every phrase and comma in order to discover the person hidden behind the words. Fr. Voillaume's words opened a door and I was then able to go in and meet this older brother who lived the Christian adventure so radically.

I came to better understand little sister Magdeleine's intuition in beginning the congregation that had become my own. Whereas the little brothers had drawn their inspiration directly from the Rule of Life written by brother Charles, meaning a monastic, cloistered way of life, she had wanted little sisters who would follow what he had actually lived in the midst of people. She justified taking her distances from what he had written by saying, "Broth-

---

23. Letter to Marie de Bondy, December 1, 1916.

er Charles of Jesus, being a living gospel, is essentially a life. Sticking only to his words would prevent the vigor of his message from rising and flowing out."[24] She immediately grasped his implicit intuition of a contemplative life *in* the world.

After final vows I was sent to Poland. I could summon no enthusiasm before that prospect. If I had joined the little sisters, it was because I wanted to live among those who were far from the Church—hardly the situation of Poland! But once again, Providence went ahead of me. In Canada, I was the last to enter the community. At the time of my final vows it had been a source of considerable anguish. How could I commit myself *forever* to a life where I might end up alone? In Poland, I encountered a region with a lot of young sisters in need of formation. Not only did I have the joy of accompanying a good number of them, but they also asked me to give the novices sessions about brother Charles. Few of his writings were translated and his whole way of thinking was so foreign to them! How could I help them enter into their inheritance? A tenderness for my sisters has always helped me on my way. I learned that it wasn't enough to just tell the story of his life, but I needed to help them discover what he could mean in their lives today. How was he guiding them in Jesus' footsteps?

I was eventually asked to come to our Generalate in Rome. I took over from little sister Annie who not only yielded up her place so graciously, but also accompanied me with a confidence that gave me wings.

Through narrating brother Charles's life so often I became familiar with the man, but a question often remained. What message did his life convey? The flesh and blood brother Charles isn't just an angel of light. When

---

24. Little sister Magdeleine to Fr. Voillaume, November 13, 1944.

you delve into his life you become familiar with his inconsistencies. He professes radical poverty but as soon as he needs something he calls on his family. He is forever quoting, "He who listens to you listens to me," to prove his obedience, but he can be as stubborn as a mule. He is prophetic in his condemnation of France's tolerance of slavery in Beni Abbès, but the prophet falls silent when he's among the slave-keeping Tuareg. I have to admit that far from discouraging me, these inconsistencies have made brother Charles even closer. His sanctity only came at the price of a lot of mistakes and humility.

In Rome we have a few souvenirs of Charles de Foucauld in a chapel that recalls Beni Abbès. Many people come to pray there and sometimes I have been asked to guide visitors. I started to ask people why they were there, what attracted them to brother Charles. Some, especially priests, commented on the importance the word *brother* held for them. Others spoke of the radical nature of his conversion and his love for the person of Jesus. For others, it was the importance he attached to Nazareth and life among the poor. Those who were interested in interreligious dialogue felt challenged by the way he labored at preparing a meeting between Islam and the gospel. Still others felt inspired by his enduring perseverance. These people helped me discover so many avenues leading to his message for us today.

I am particularly fond of a letter he wrote to his fifteen-year-old nephew and godson Charles de Blic. Brother Charles had hoped that he would become a priest, but he received a letter from his nephew announcing his decision to join the Navy. Here is his answer:

> My dear Charles, thank you for your kind letter, your wishes and your prayers . . . mostly for your prayers because your letter only goes as far as me whereas your prayers go all the way to God. . . . My dearest, if

you want to be a sailor, you must like long journeys, faraway journeys; you must therefore have a lively taste for prayer which in only one instant leads you so far, so high! No sailboat or steamliner will ever lead you as far as a minute of prayer! The journeys of our soul to God reach further than any ocean; and while the discoveries sailors make are limited, as is this globe, the discoveries made by the soul as it rises through prayer to God have no boundaries because God is infinite. . . . The spaces that separate the creature from the Creator are vaster than the seas and there is matter for longer journeys. And the discoveries one makes are always more enchanting, because everything we glimpse of God is divinely beautiful; there are no deserted, feverish, burnt, or frozen shores: everything is always breathtakingly divine.

So you see my dearest that I do travel and go on wonderful journeys without ever leaving the foot of the altar. There are more mysteries in the little Tabernacle than there are on the bottom of the ocean floor or surface of the earth, and more beauty than in the whole of creation. My dearest, a recluse goes on wonderful journeys, way beyond the earth, while staying deep in his hermitage. Centuries ago he found the hot air balloon and the means for rising up above the atmosphere and beyond the stars.

My darling, may JESUS make you sail toward Him and may He make you into a saint. I embrace you and love you in His divine Heart,

Br Ch. of Jesus

Let us also enter into our explorer-brother's hot air balloon. May he reveal to us those stars that guided his ascension and that today can cast light on our arid pathways toward the one he liked to call his "Beloved Brother and Lord."

3

From Emptiness to Presence: Turning Religion into Love

"We have believed in love."[25]

When Charles de Foucauld was searching for his vocation, Fr. Huvelin sent him to the Benedictines in Solesmes with a letter of introduction in which he wrote that Charles was someone who "turned religion into love." These few words are an admirable appreciation of the man. He would never seek security in religion. It would always be a question of self-surrender.

After his conversion, people who knew him started noticing a change. The president of the Geographical Society of Paris wrote to his secretary, "I have a sincere affection for Mr. de Foucauld. He's a brilliant man. But I'm afraid he's either contracted some illness or is suffering from emotional instability. I take the liberty of writing you this . . . because he deserves to be treated with care."[26] But Ibn Arabi, a Muslim mystic from the twelfth century, had long ago given the diagnosis: "The one whose sickness is called Jesus will never know healing."

An existential crisis

In order to fully understand Charles de Foucauld's conversion, one needs to consider the void he had experienced as a young person. The Love he encountered would be com-

---

25. See 1 John 4:16.
26. Henri Duveyrier to Charles Maunoir, February 18, 1888.

mensurate with the emptiness he had endured. The loss of his parents meant that he was raised by his grandfather. Friends and family recall a very bright but insecure child. Marie de Bondy said, "His grandfather was very fond of him but he contributed greatly to making him what's known as a spoilt child." François Geny gave a brief testimony for his cause for beatification, saying, "I wasn't the same age as Father de Foucauld, who seemed a bit strange and unsociable at the time." Opinions are nonetheless unanimous in recalling that he was "very gifted and exceptionally bright."[27]

As a young child, he was introduced to the faith by a *saintly mother*, but after her death he remained alone. "Children are thrown into the world before receiving the arms they need to combat the enemies they meet both inside and outside of themselves, enemies which assail them as they enter their teenage years."[28]

The *enemy outside* would be the climate of rationalism that reigned in France during the second half of the nineteenth century, to which he addressed his thirst for knowledge. The spectacular progress of science and its industrial applications favored the emergence of a skeptical attitude to religion. His teachers in Nancy were all steeped in that line of thought. His eleventh grade teacher, Mr. Jules Duvaux, was Minister of Public Instruction in 1882-83, during the rise of anticlericalism. It is hardly surprising that to a fifteen-year-old, faith seemed "incompatible with common sense."[29] He would later recall, "To me, the faith one could place in such different religions seemed the condemnation of them all. My child-

---

27. Georges de Latouche to Oscar MacCarthy, May 14, 1883.
28. Letter to Marie de Bondy, December 10, 1897.
29. Letter to Henri Duveyrier, February 21, 1892.

hood faith seemed no more acceptable than the others, with its 1=3 that made no sense at all."[30]

The *enemy within* came from his own brilliant mind. He would later confess to his cousin Marie de Bondy that "there were no controls and I read a lot of inappropriate things." His school friend Gabriel Tourdes was his reading companion. Recalling the past, Charles wrote to him when he was twenty:

> Do you remember the Easter holidays when I stayed in the little house? I would spend the morning in bed, smoking my hookah. You would come in the morning, take your seat on the big sofa or walk around the room, and we would talk. You would read out loud while I washed. We would stay together until lunch, and most of the time even later than that, because I often kept you until 9 pm.[31]

Their reading list was impressive: Greek and Latin classics, poetry, Enlightenment authors, skeptics, and anticlericals. "Unfortunately, we unlearned how to pray to God together."[32] He wrote to Gabriel, "You have to admit that the Elysian Fields are just as good as that smoky heaven full of incense where the elect sit around forever just playing the harp and singing the Lord's praises until the end of time."[33]

Even though he didn't say it directly, his inability to believe was far from being a matter of indifference to him. A latent anxiety pervades many of his letters. In order to prepare their list of reading for the holidays Charles wrote to Gabriel:

---

30. Letter to Henri de Castries, August 14, 1901.
31. Letter to Gabriel Tourdes, April 13, 1878.
32. Letter to Gabriel Tourdes, May 11, 1891.
33. Letter to Gabriel Tourdes, April 13, 1878.

Dear old Tourdes, I haven't written to you for ages.
. . . We have 10 days of holiday at Easter. I arrive in
Nancy Friday morning around 6:30. You can look up
the exact time, knowing that I leave Paris at 9:35 pm. I
warn you that I'm counting on you every evening. We
are going to continue our rampage through books. I'm
mad with joy at the thought of going back to Nancy
for a few days. I plan to enjoy myself completely
using all that gives pleasure to body and mind.[34]

In October 1874, he was sent to a boarding school
run by the Jesuits in Paris. He was sixteen years old and
sorely missed home. In his first letter to Gabriel he wrote,
"You are lucky. I often say it and I think it even more often. Me, I'm infinitely bored. I say it often and I think it
all the time."[35] He put a lot of pressure on his grandfather
to bring him home to Nancy.

I hurt my poor grandfather so much when I was at
school at rue des Postes. I refused to work, to the
extent that by February, I still hadn't cut the pages of
my geometry textbook. I was supposed to have been
studying it daily since November. I would write him
every other day, letters that were sometimes up to 40
pages long, begging him to take me back to Nancy,
and all the rest which you can imagine and which
was the result of such turmoil.[36]

Boredom resurfaces in his letters from Saint-Cyr
where he was studying to be an officer. "My dear Tourdes,
heartfelt thanks for your letter. Write to me often. It's always a joy to receive letters when you're bored, and I'm

---

34. Letter to Gabriel Tourdes, March 27, 1877.
35. Letter to Gabriel Tourdes, October 21, 1874.
36. Letter to Marie de Bondy, November 8, 1893.

absolutely bored to death here."[37] His boredom only increased the next year. "It's very sad to no longer be able to read as we did in the past, to have nothing for recreation but theory and vile publications about fortifications, artillery etc. It all reeks of barbarity."[38]

His despondency deepened with his grandfather's death during his second year at Saint-Cyr. He called it an "immense sorrow,"[39] because it awakened childhood wounds. He camouflaged the pain by a wild lifestyle, financed by his inheritance. He and his roommate were often under house arrest. Their room was famous for the excellent dinners brought in by caterers, and long card games organized to keep the captives company. In spite of his putting on a brave face, anxiety would resurface whenever he was alone. He wrote to Gabriel:

> You're lucky about one thing. It's that when you're tired of having fun you can go back to your family and live quietly and contentedly with your relatives and your books. For me it's different. In one fell swoop I have lost my family, my home, my tranquility and that carefree living I cherished. It's lost forever. I will never again be as light-hearted and content as I was in Nancy, in the good old days when we were together so often.[40]

At twenty years old he saw no future for himself. His letters to Gabriel were a reflection of what he was going through.

---

37. Letter to Gabriel Tourdes, November 23, 1877.
38. Ibid.
39. Letter to Henri Duveyrier, February 21, 1892.
40. Letter to Gabriel Tourdes, December 1978.

My dear old Tourdes, I hope that you are happier than I right now as I write to you. I'm sitting at my old desk, in my old armchair where you saw me so often . . . I would never have thought I would miss our teenage years so much. My letters all seem like complaints: you must be fed up. It's not that I write to you all that often, because I'm behind in my correspondence with you. I'm like those who only pray to God when they are very sick: I only write to you when I am very sad. Sincerely yours, Charles.[41]

An emptiness full of presence

Things started to change from the moment he first set foot in Algeria as a young soldier. The Arab world enchanted him. Eight months spent under a tent in South Oran when he was twenty-three made him decide to change careers, and he quit the army to go travelling. During his year-long exploration of Morocco, as he trekked from village to village, he was often welcomed in *zaouias*, centers of the Muslim brotherhoods. Contrary to the complicated arithmetic of the Trinity, "Islamism pleased me a great deal with its simplicity: dogmatic simplicity, hierarchic simplicity, moral simplicity."[42]

The desert, a space which was in harmony with his own soul, had left its stamp on this imposing and austere religion. His account of his arrival in Tisint, one of the biggest oases in the Moroccan Sahara, reveals his sensitivity to Islamic mysticism:

We slowly wind our way along a thousand canals amidst lofty palm trees that take on a surreal

---

41. Letter to Gabriel Tourdes, December 1978.
42. Letter to Henri de Castries, August 14, 1901.

appearance in the moonlight. Their silvery branches cast thick shadows over us as we approach the *ksar*. We catch sight of the whole village with its storied, whitewashed houses at the foot of the gleaming bluff whose polished rock glistens this magical evening. On this cloudless night, the moon's soft gleam lights up the whole scene. The air is warm and still. Amid the deep tranquility of these enchanted surroundings, I arrive at my first stop in the Sahara. The serenity of such nights makes you understand the belief Arabs have in a mysterious night, *leïla el qedr*, when the heavens open and the angels come down to earth, when sea water becomes fresh and all of nature bows to adore its Creator.[43]

He later wrote to an officer friend who confessed to having been seduced by Islam, "Islam made a very deep impression on me. The sight of such faith, of people living continually in the presence of God, gave me an insight into something greater and truer than worldly pursuits: *ad majora nati sumus.*"[44] The awareness of having been born for *greater things* echoes the call that continually rings from the top of minarets: *Allahu akbar.* God is greater. Islam awoke in him the question, *"Who am I?"* and hinted that an answer could only be found if he considered the One who is greater. He needed to ask him, *"Who are you?"* Meeting Islam clarified a question that he carried within, of which he was unaware. And this question would not go away.

---

43. Charles de Foucauld, *Reconnaissance au Maroc*, Paris, Société d'éditions géographiques, maritimes et coloniales, 1939, p. 219.
44. *"We are born for greater things."* Letter to Henri de Castries, July 8, 1901.

After returning to Paris to publish the results of his exploration, Charles began an anguished search for truth. He spoke of a *tormented soul* and *anxiety*. In this search, hunger would prove to be his best ally. As in the case of the prodigal son, it would help him enter into himself. "Your first grace, the one I see as the dawn of my conversion, was to have made me hungry, a famine that was both physical and spiritual."[45]

Hunger was the voice of God searching for him in his faraway country. After his conversion, he would always keep a double memory of his wayward years, remembering them not just in order to ask for forgiveness but also to give thanks.

> You made me feel a painful emptiness, a sadness the likes of which I never felt before or since. It came over me every night when I went home to my lodgings. What we called parties left me silent and heavy-hearted. I would organize them but when the time came I would fall silent, feeling only disgust and infinite boredom. You gave me the vague restlessness of a troubled conscience, for though my conscience was asleep it was not altogether dead and that was enough to create a feeling of discontent that poisoned my life. I have never felt that sadness, that discontent, that restlessness at any time but then. It must have been your gift, my God. I was so far from suspecting it. How good you are![46]

The restlessness he felt opened him to the witness given by his family. He was very sensitive to the way they welcomed him after his return from his faraway country.

---

45. Meditations on Luke 15:11-32, Nazareth, March 1898.
46. Notes during retreat in Nazareth, November 8, 1897.

He guessed that there was some connection between their attitude and their faith.

> I told myself that this religion might not be so absurd after all and I started going to church, without believing. It was only there that I felt at ease, spending long hours repeating this strange prayer: "My God, if you exist, then let me know you!" The idea came to me that I needed to find out about this religion. Perhaps I might discover the truth I had despaired of ever finding.[47]

With Charles, God's absence is full of his presence. As the Little Prince said, "What makes the desert beautiful is that, somewhere, it hides a well."[48] Charles prayed even before he believed.

The man who learned how to kneel

His thirst for truth first steered him towards ancient moralists, but what he found left him cold. He intuitively felt that there existed a form of knowledge other than rationalism, and finally he said to his cousin: "You're so lucky to believe! I am searching for light and cannot find it." She answered him, "Do you think searching all alone is the right way to go about it?"[49] She directed him towards Fr. Huvelin, who would be the father and friend he needed so much. Right from the beginning, his journey to God led him to other people. The God we find all on our own risks being one in our own image

---

47. Letter to Henri de Castries, August 14, 1901.
48. Antoine de Saint Exupéry, *The Little Prince*, New York: Harbrace Paperbound Library, 1943, p. 93.
49. cf. *Summarium* of Diocesan Inquest, p. 125-126.

and likeness, and so we miss the encounter with the God who is *greater*.

Resolved to ask for religion lessons, Charles approached Fr. Huvelin's confessional at the end of October 1886. A graduate of the *Ecole Normale Superieure*, the latter was more than qualified to answer his questions, but he also had a gift for sensing what was going on in someone's soul. This young man's feverish search needed to move to another level. God isn't an idea you seize hold of but someone you meet. Even if Charles claimed not to be a believer, Fr. Huvelin invited him to go to confession.

Charles wrote several accounts of his conversion but he never explained why he made the decision to get down on his knees. Perhaps he suddenly experienced in the depths of his soul that his "body had been meant and made for the act of kneeling."[50] Hunger had turned him into a poor man. He would later say that, "If there is rejoicing in heaven over a sinner who repents, there was plenty of joy on the day I entered that confessional . . . I cannot help crying whenever I remember."[51] The Truth for which he had yearned was not an idea but a person, and from his merciful womb Charles was born into a new world.

> Those who live by faith have their souls full of new ideas, new pleasures, new principles. New horizons open out in front of them, marvelous horizons illumined by a heavenly light whose beauty comes from the beauty of God. Absorbed in these new truths that the world has no notions of, believers have no choice but to start a new life. Anyone who

---

50. Etty Hillesum, Klaas A. D. Smelik (ed.), *Etty: The Letters and Diaries of Etty Hillesum 1941-1943*, Grand Rapids: Wm. B. Eerdmans Publishing, 2002, p. 320.

51. Meditations on Luke 15:11-32, Nazareth, March 1898.

sees this light and takes it at its true value holds it infinitely important, clings to it unshakeably, follows it in everything and refuses to be turned aside by anything.[52]

Fr. Huvelin immediately had him make his second *first Communion*. If hunger was the deciding factor that brought him back to faith, the Eucharist was nourishment that could satisfy him. His love for the Eucharist has its origins in his conversion experience, and those origins would accompany him throughout life. It is what is expressed by his logo *Jesus Caritas*. The Sacred Heart is the icon of the person he met on the day of his conversion. One of the first phrases he learned to say in Tamahaq was, "This heart drawn on my robe is there so that I remember God and human beings in order to love them." From the Love that came to meet him, he drew his own love for people.

The Sacred Heart: a spirituality of love and confidence

Brother Charles often thanked his cousin Marie for introducing him to the mystery of the Sacred Heart. His cousin's love allowed him to discover a *greater* love that was channeled through Jesus' human heart. "What have heaven and myself, such perfection and my misery, in common? . . . your heart, my Lord Jesus, your heart which binds two such opposite things together."[53] He painted a life-sized image of the Sacred Heart for his chapel in Beni Abbès, "stretching out His arms in order to embrace, welcome, call all people and give Himself for them all by

---

52. Notes during retreat in Nazareth, 9 November 9, 1897.
53. Ibid.

offering His heart."[54] He wanted representations of the Sacred Heart that shone with plenty of rays. At the time of his ordination he wrote very precise instructions to his cousin who was embroidering him a chasuble:

> Thank you for making a chasuble for your son. I will be very moved to wear it. Try to make it all white except for the pink heart, the little brown cross, flames all around the cross that emerges from the heart and yellow rays shining all around. Make a heart that shines brightly. May it shine out over this poor earth, over all those we love and over ourselves.[55]

Fr. Huvelin, who was fond of repeating St. John's phrase, *Credidimus caritati*,[56] encouraged Charles to build his life on love by not concentrating on himself but rather allowing love to take hold of him, just as he was. It gave him a sense of confidence that underpinned his whole life and allowed him to dare a great deal. In 1893 when he first expressed to Fr. Huvelin his idea of founding a congregation, he wrote, "What gives me courage to undertake something which is so contrary to my sinfulness and misery is that Our Lord said that if you had sinned a lot you needed to love a lot."[57] He would not succeed in everything, but his confidence would be unshakeable. He would try to pass it on to others. To Louis Massignon, who was tormented by his homosexual orientation, he wrote:

> Peace and confidence, hope. Don't turn in on yourself. Our wretchedness is a mire which should

---

54. Letter to Marie de Bondy, January 7, 1902.
55. Letter to Marie de Bondy, September 20, 1900.
56. "We have believed in love"; see 1 John 4:16.
57. Letter to Fr. Huvelin, September 22, 1893.

often provoke our humility, but it isn't something on which we should focus our attention. We should turn our gaze so much more towards the Beloved, towards that infinite, uncreated love that deigns to cherish us. . . . When you love, you forget about yourself and you think about the one you love. To only meditate how unworthy you are isn't to love.[58]

This attitude of confidence would not just be toward God but toward people as well. One need only think of his settlement in Tamanrasset, where his only security rested on the word of a Tuareg chief who had only recently given his submission to the French.

During his youth, Charles couldn't accept the mystery of a God who was one in three Persons, and yet that mystery would consume his life. The mystery of the Trinity says that at the heart of God there is ecstasy, going out toward the other. And it's in this exodus that Charles became a happy man. Love came to meet him when he was twenty-eight, and as it was in his nature to do, he responded to it radically, turning religion into a *great* love.

In his letters as a young man, Charles often expressed feelings of emptiness and boredom. They are a striking contrast to the letter he wrote to Gabriel Tourdes from Beni Abbès in 1902.

Dear friend, were your heart to tell you to come and visit me, you know with what joy I would welcome you and share my cell with you. You would be served the best barley loaves and the finest dates. We would talk about the past, about the present which is better still, and about the future which shall be yet more delightful. . . . I am a happy man, very happy,

---

58. Letter to Louis Massignon, Easter 1912.

extremely happy even though I haven't been seeking happiness for many years now.[59]

The Word

Brother Charles's life testifies to a deep personal friendship with Jesus, but it would be wrong to think that it was something that came to him easily. In the words of St. Teresa of Avila, whom he counted among his "mothers," one needed a *determinación determinada* in order to follow the Lord. "Love doesn't consist in feeling that we love but in wanting to love; when you want to love above all else, you do in fact love above all else," he wrote. "To feel that we love Him and that He loves us would be paradise. And except for a few rare moments, paradise isn't for here below."[60] Tender emotions aren't enough.

In a life that would meander along many detours and through many deserts, it was at the table of the Word and the Eucharist that he would seek stability in love.

Having left the Trappists, brother Charles lived as a hermit for three and a half years in Nazareth. Even if he wrote to his brother-in-law that he was now settled in a *delightful hermitage*, one mustn't be deceived. A man of his stamina wasn't going to find it easy to be locked up in a little shed all day long! A few months later his prayer was feeling the effects of his enclosure: "Aridity and darkness. Everything is difficult: holy communion, prayers, meditations, everything, everything, even to tell Jesus that I love Him. I need to cling to my life of faith. If at least I felt that Jesus loves me . . . but He never says so."[61] The well was dry and he was going to have to dig deeper.

---

59. Letter to Gabriel Tourdes, March 7, 1902.
60. Letter to Louis Massignon, July 15, 1916.
61. Notebook, June 6, 1897.

Fr. Huvelin again took up his role as Charles's spiritual director and replied, "My dear child, put your meditations into writing—it's a very good habit in and of itself—and in your case it will help clarify things and settle your spirit."[62] This practice did indeed help him a great deal, but it doesn't always help those who try to read him! Charles wasn't a man who did things halfway, and he wrote thousands of pages! Today all of it has been published, although he himself only ever wanted a short brochure printed. He had entitled it *The Only Model*. It was a portrait of Jesus made up entirely of Gospel quotations grouped around certain virtues.

In a letter where he narrated his conversion, brother Charles wrote, "Everyone knows that the first effect of love is imitation."[63] That statement can surprise us, but what he meant was that he who loved Jesus would want to follow in his footsteps. "Your Rule is to follow me . . . do what I would do. In all things ask yourself, 'What would Our Lord have done?' And do it. It's your only rule, but it's an absolute one."[64] Imitation became the key to his spirituality.

His meditations always began with looking at Jesus and then he drew the consequences for himself. What should he do in order to imitate what he saw? Imitation wasn't just a matter of effort, because the Word of God has a transformative power in and of itself. Little by little he would be fashioned into the image of his elder brother, Jesus.

Aside from the training he had received as a Trappist, brother Charles's religious formation by and large took place outside of established structures. At a time when seminaries relied on the scholastic approach or when the

---

62. Fr. Huvelin to Charles de Foucauld, May 24, 1897.
63. Letter to Henri de Castries, August 14, 1901.
64. Notebook, June 6, 1897.

modernist crisis made people wary of the Bible, he drew his inspiration directly from the Word of God. "The Gospel showed me that the first commandment was to love God with all one's heart and that everything needed to begin and end with love."[65] Brother Charles's first disciples were very struck by the evangelical freshness that emanated from his life. On reading his biography, which first appeared in 1921, little sister Magdeleine said, "In him I had at last found everything that I dreamed about doing in life—the Gospel in action, total poverty, a love for lowliness but above all love in the fullest sense of the word: Jesus-Caritas, Jesus-Love."[66]

The Bread

His love for the *Only Model* was not only fed at the table of the Word, but also at the table of the Eucharist, where Jesus makes himself present. Hunger led brother Charles to his conversion and it would remain his guide on a journey of conversion that would last a lifetime.

The eucharistic mystery has many aspects, but what struck brother Charles above all was the dimension of *presence*. He was very physical in his understanding of *the Real Presence* and this has attracted some criticism from theologians. He would write, "O my Lord Jesus, you are present in the Eucharist! You are there, only one meter away from me in the Tabernacle!"[67] He didn't sufficiently discern that it's the presence of Jesus' *risen Body*, a Body which isn't subject to the laws of physics. It is faith that

65. Letter to Henri de Castries, August 14, 1901.
66. Annie of Jesus, *Little Sister Magdeleine of Jesus: Message of Bethlehem to a Suffering World*, Bangalore: Claretian Publications, 2010, p. 27.
67. Notes during retreat in Nazareth, November 7, 1897.

renders him close, not the number of meters. His simplistic logic can sometimes make us smile! From Beni Abbès he wrote to his cousin:

> Evenings are so calm and nights so serene under this vast sky with its wide horizons, bright with stars. They are so peaceful and their silent song permeates you with a sense of the Eternal, the Infinite, the Beyond. You could spend the whole night just contemplating them. And yet after only a few moments I cut that contemplation short and return to the Tabernacle; because there is more in the humble Tabernacle. Everything is nothing compared to the Beloved.[68]

On the eve of his ordination at the age of forty-two, brother Charles was very moved to think that he was going to have the right to touch the Lord's Body. At the time, Communion was received on the tongue and, except for a priest, no one could touch the host. Someone who was present at his ordination witnessed the interest he aroused in all present. They knew that he was a Viscount who had undertaken a daring exploration of Morocco. In spite of their efforts to get him to talk on that subject, he would only lower his gaze saying, "Tomorrow I shall hold Our Lord between my fingers."

A sexual dimension is not absent in the eucharistic words: "This is my body given for you." It did not escape brother Charles's attention. During the retreat before his diaconate he read the story of Esther, drawing a parallel between the stages leading to ordination and the progressive rights of the fiancée to the body of the beloved: to *see* it, to *touch* it from time to time, to have *unlimited access* to it. The words *Spouse* and *Beloved* appear so often when he refers to Jesus that one remembers what

---

68. Letter to Marie de Bondy, September 12, 1902.

Fr. Huvelin said about him: "He turns religion into love." He integrated his affectivity into his understanding of the rights priesthood gave him to the Body of the Beloved, and it helped him retain the youthfulness of his love.

His sensitivity to this dimension of *presence* made him fond of praying before the Blessed Sacrament exposed. He wrote that this presence was given to us:

> Out of love, for our good, to make us warm, fervent, loving and tender because we are frigid; to make us strong and courageous because we are weak; to give us hope and confidence because we are downhearted; to make us happy because we are sad and discouraged.[69]

Adoration of the exposed Blessed Sacrament was obviously not a form of prayer known to the early Christians, but it evolved over time, especially with the quarrels regarding the Real Presence in the sixteenth century. In brother Charles's day, liturgical rules concerning exposition of the Blessed Sacrament required that at least three adorers be present for a minimum of eight hours. Brother Charles would rarely be able to meet those conditions. Sometimes Abd-Jesu, a three-year-old slave child he had redeemed, and an old blind woman who resided at the Fraternity in Beni Abbès, would be enlisted as adorers! He wrote to his cousin:

> I will do all I can, calling on the help of poor Marie and Abd-Jesu so that I can expose the Blessed Sacrament on Easter. I can no longer expose it since the departure of Peter and Paul due to lack of adorers. Sorry for my chicken scratch. Apart from the fact that

---

69. Meditation on Luke 9:16 during retreat in Ephrem, March 18, 1898.

I usually scribble quickly and badly, at this moment Abd-Jesu is hanging onto my neck, nibbling away at my ears. Since I'm his only playmate, I have to let him do it. He's as happy as a lark, which is to his credit, since I'm his only companion.[70]

The mystery of the Presence he adored in the chapel and the apostolate of presence he lived among the men and women of the Sahara were not separable.

A spirituality of presence

What does *presence* mean? As human beings, it's in our moments of fragility that we can perceive with greater clarity what we are. A newborn infant deprived of its mother's presence experiences distress. Likewise, a dying person wishes nothing other than presence. It is our most basic need. In his passion, Jesus reveals that his greatest suffering came from feeling abandoned. That's why his mother was there . . . standing. Presence saves us from solitude. That can be forgotten in a world that values power more than relationships. "Being a savior with Jesus," to use a phrase dear to brother Charles's heart, means to place presence at the center of our life, to invest in relationship. Adoration of the Blessed Sacrament leads us in that direction. It takes us out of a world ruled by efficiency into one governed by gratuitousness.

Before entering the Trappists, brother Charles wrote a note to his cousin, telling her his reasons for entering religious life. "Fr. Huvelin told me many things and we clarified once again why I wanted to enter religious life. It's to keep Our Lord company, especially in His sufferings."[71]

---

70. Letter to Marie de Bondy, March 30, 1903.
71. Letter to Marie de Bondy, September 20, 1889.

Brother Charles often spoke of his desire to "keep Our Lord company," and it summarizes his life. He does qualify it, however, by saying, "in His sufferings." The Gospels helped him discover that Jesus continues to suffer in the least of his brothers and sisters. Charles wrote to his nephew, "When a poor or sick person knocks at the door, it's to Jesus that I run to open because 'what you do to one of the least of these you do to me.'"[72] This line of thinking took him far. Following his retreat in 1903 he wrote his resolutions on Ash Wednesday: "Promised to employ all the instants of my life to save Our Lord who is being lost in all the lost souls." What he writes recalls Etty Hillesum's insight, that in order to save God you need to save human beings.

A few months before his death brother Charles wrote to Louis Massignon:

> I think there is no saying in the Gospel that made a deeper impression on me and more transformed my life than this one: "Whatsoever you did to one of the least of these you did it to me." If we remember that these are the words of Uncreated Truth and come from the same lips that said, "This is my Body, this is my Blood," how compellingly we are moved to seek out Jesus and love Him in the "least," the sinners, the poor.[73]

Written at the end of his life, these words express the synthesis of his spiritual adventure, following his One Lord present in both the sacrament of the poor and the sacrament of the altar. They are the legacy he leaves his disciples, the foundation of a contemplative life in the world of the poor.

---

72. Letter to Charles de Blic, June 16, 1902.
73. Letter to Louis Massignon, August 1, 1916.

4

Nazareth:
Finding God in Everyday Life

The Bible is often as eloquent in its omissions as it is in its words. Rabbis like to say that the white spaces surrounding each letter speak because they make the word comprehensible. This must be true regarding Nazareth because the Old Testament never mentions it. One of the principle reasons for Jesus' rejection by the religious establishment was his origins. Nazareth was an insignificant village. When Nicodemus sought to defend him, he was told, "Search and you will see that no prophet is to rise from Galilee."[74] During the Deuteronomic Reform, great pains had been taken to purify worship by centering it in Jerusalem. Nazareth, which lay at the crossroads with the pagan world, was far away in every sense of the word. "Can anything good come out of Nazareth?"[75] Nathanael's question isn't just addressed to Philip, because Nazareth is the shell enclosing most of our lives. Do we discover the pearl within it?

Nazareth is an extension of the scandal of the Incarnation, a little house where God lives together with human beings as a family. God's desire for intimacy is much harder to accept than we might think. Shamed by their nakedness, Adam and Eve hid among the trees of the garden when they heard him approaching. In Nazareth, God again drew near, but more unobtrusively. And it's toward this little house that Charles would advance to meet him. By making Nazareth his home the Viscount

---

74. John 7:52
75. John 1:46

53

de Foucauld would receive his true title of nobility: *little brother of Jesus.*

Going down to Nazareth

After leaving Fr. Huvelin's confessional, Charles relived the experience of the early Christians. "Now when they heard this they were cut to the heart, and said to Peter and the rest of the apostles, 'Brethren, what shall we do?'"[76]

Very quickly he expressed a desire to enter religious life, but being a wise mentor, Fr. Huvelin made him wait. Sensing his need to see and touch, he suggested that Charles go on pilgrimage to the Holy Land. Even though he would later say that he went only out of obedience, for Charles, as for many saints, this pilgrimage would be a turning point.

He set off with words from a sermon by Fr. Huvelin indelibly engraved in his soul: "Jesus took the lowest place so utterly that no one has ever been able to get it away from him."[77] In the parable on choosing places at table (see Luke 14:7-14), guests are invited to make their way to *the lowest place.* But in his sermon, Fr. Huvelin applies it to Jesus himself. If Charles wished to keep Jesus company, he needed to make his way to *the lowest place.*

He arrived in the Holy Land just before Christmas and went to Bethlehem. Jesus was born in a stable because there was no room for him in the city of David. Laid in a manger, he indeed began his life in the lowest place. Charles then went to Jerusalem, where he contemplated Jesus who had also ended his life in the lowest place, crucified between two thieves. From there he made his way

---

76. Acts 2:37
77. Annie of Jesus, *Charles de Foucauld: In the Footsteps of Jesus of Nazareth*, London: New City Press, 2004, p. 45.

to Galilee. At the time Nazareth was a little town under Turkish occupation. According to the Liévin Guide (1869), the streets were narrow, dirty, and often soiled with manure. As he walked Nazareth's alleyways, Charles realized that it wasn't just at the beginning and the end of his life that Jesus had taken the lowest place, but every day. It was a shock, and a call. If it was among Muslims that he gained the insight that he was born *for greater things*, it was in Nazareth that he discovered he could only reach them if he went down. It was in going down that he could be raised up to God.

In his book *The God of Jesus Christ*, Joseph Ratzinger wrote:

> While sentimentalism about Nazareth was still flourishing, the true mystery of Nazareth's real content was discovered in a new way—and people living at the time knew nothing about it. In his search for the "last place," Charles de Foucauld discovered Nazareth. . . . Nazareth has a permanent message for the Church. The New Covenant did not begin in the Temple nor on the holy mountain; it began in the little dwelling of the Virgin, the house of the worker, and one of the forgotten places of "pagan Galilee" from which no good could be expected.[78]

It was because of Nazareth that Charles became a Trappist. "I didn't feel I was made for preaching like Jesus in His public life, so I needed to imitate Him in His hidden life as a poor and humble workman at Nazareth. I thought nothing would offer me this way of life better

---

78. Joseph Ratzinger, *The God of Jesus Christ: Meditations on God in the Trinity*, Chicago: Franciscan Herald Press, 1979, p. 69-71.

than a Trappist monastery."[79] It was also because of Nazareth that he left the Trappists seven years later.

In a life that would meander a great deal, Nazareth always remained the stable element. He meditated on Nazareth from the outset, and was still reflecting on the same subject a few months before his death when he wrote: "'He went down with them and came to Nazareth.' His whole life long He did nothing other than go down: go down by His Incarnation, go down by becoming a little child, go down by obeying, go down by becoming poor, forsaken, exiled, persecuted, tortured, placing Himself always at the lowest place."[80]

Brother Charles found a synthesis of Jesus' life in the words "go down." He wrote to a Trappist friend, "I think it's my vocation: to go down."[81] He drew the consequences for himself in a statement that was typical of his radical nature: "As for me, always seek the lowest of the low places, so as to be as little as my master, to be with Him, to walk behind Him, step by step, as a faithful servant, a faithful disciple."[82]

To grow in Nazareth

Brother Charles's insight regarding Nazareth is deeply rooted in the gospel. St. Luke writes that Jesus *went down* to Nazareth. The scene of Jesus' finding in the Temple is framed by two references to Nazareth, both of which say that it was a place where he grew.

---

79. Letter to Henri de Castries, August 14, 1901.
80. Meditation on Luke 2:50-51, March 20, 1916.
81. Letter to Fr. Jerome, January 24, 1897.
82. Notes from a retreat in Nazareth, November 6, 1897.

> *And when they had performed everything according to the law of the Lord, they returned into Galilee, to their own city, **Nazareth**. And the child **grew** and became strong, filled with **wisdom**; and the **favor** of God was upon him.*

Now his parents went to Jerusalem every year at the feast of the Passover. And when he was twelve years old, they went up according to custom; and when the feast was ended, as they were returning, the boy Jesus stayed behind in Jerusalem. His parents did not know it, but supposing him to be in the company they went a day's journey, and they sought him among their kinsfolk and acquaintances; and when they did not find him, they returned to Jerusalem, seeking him. After three days they found him in the temple, sitting among the teachers. . . . And when they saw him they were astonished; and his mother said to him, "Son, why have you treated us so? Behold, your father and I have been looking for you anxiously." And he said to them, "How is it that you sought me? Did you not know that I must be in my Father's house?" And they did not understand the saying which he spoke to them.

> *And he went down with them and came to **Nazareth**, and was obedient to them; and his mother kept all these things in her heart. And Jesus **increased in wisdom** and in stature, and in **favor** with God and man.*[83]

Luke's pericope about the finding in the Temple has the story of the child Samuel in the background. In verse 52 Luke adapts 1 Samuel 2:26: "Now the boy Samuel

---

83. Luke 2:39-52, emphases added.

continued to grow both in stature and in favor both with the Lord and with men." It was through living day and night in the Lord's presence at the sanctuary in Shiloh that Samuel grew. Jesus, on the contrary, grew in favor with God and people by *leaving* the sanctuary and living in the company of parents who did not understand him. The encounter between his greatness and our poverty enriched him.

Sandwiched between two mentions of Nazareth, the finding in the Temple casts light on its deep meaning. The key phrase in the scene is Jesus' insistence that he *must be in his Father's house*. The logical conclusion would have been that he needed to stay in Jerusalem, but we are told that he went down to Nazareth. In doing this, Jesus was *about his Father's business*. Both before and after the Temple incident, Jesus' life seems to have been the same, but the meaning had changed. By going down to Nazareth and living under his parents' authority, Jesus was *in his Father's house*. Luke reveals that glory is the interior lining of life in Nazareth, because God is there. It is up to us, then, to discover the glory hidden in the little things. It's something Toyohiko Kagawa, a Japanese Christian pacifist, was keenly aware of when he wrote:

> Whether you wet your hands in the water-basin, fan the fire with the bamboo bellows, set down endless columns of figures at a desk, labour in the rice-fields with your head in the burning sun and your feet in the mud, or stand at work before the smelting furnace, so long as you do not do all this with just the same religiousness as if you were monks praying in a monastery, the world will never be saved.[84]

---

84. René Voillaume, *Seeds of the Desert*, Chicago: Fides Publishers, 1955, p. 140.

The Incarnation made daily human reality a sacred space, a meeting place with God. To live Nazareth is to dialogue with the Son of Man about little things, allowing him to give meaning to our life, to all life. In this dialogue everything takes on importance, not because we do great things but because we speak about these little things with the One who gives importance to everything.

During his pilgrimage, it was not in the silence of a chapel but while walking the streets of Nazareth that Charles experienced a kind of theophany. Dissatisfied after seven years as a Trappist, he wrote to his cousin: "I am longing to lead at last the life I've been looking for these seven years and more. I glimpsed it, guessed at it, as I was walking the streets of Nazareth where the feet of Our Lord had trod, a poor tradesman lost in extreme lowliness and obscurity."[85] He spent all of his life searching for what he had glimpsed that day. The mystery of Nazareth would gradually reveal itself to him, but only at the price of a great deal of searching and mistakes. Each discovery would lead him on to something new, but more than once he had to sell all he possessed in order to buy the pearl of great price.

Nazareth: A place where you live with Jesus

Some of Charles de Foucauld's disciples speak of *Nazareth* as a spirituality lived out "at the heart of the masses," to use the French title of René Voillaume's influential book. But that was not the primary meaning Charles attributed to Nazareth, at least not initially. For him, it was a life of silence shared with the Holy Family. It was the setting for his life in God.

---

85. Letter to Marie de Bondy, June 24, 1896.

Holy Virgin, St. Joseph, take me with you, hold me close, hide me between you as your little child at the feet of Our Lord. Make me share your tranquil and blessed nights of contemplation . . . and then spend my days in your company. During the day your souls remained absorbed in His divine contemplation and despite your various occupations your eyes were always turned in adoration towards Jesus.[86]

Having returned from his pilgrimage to the Holy Land, it was natural that if Charles de Foucauld wanted to live his Nazareth spirituality he should look towards contemplative orders. At the time, people imagined that the Holy Family had lived in perpetual silence and adoration around the God-child, eating only the absolute minimum and speaking "as little as possible." In this regard, many of brother Charles's meditations could make us smile. He says to Jesus, "You have given me a life of prayer, of reading, of humble work where I talk a bit, but very little, and where I eat, but not much, poorly, simply: it's your Nazareth life, recollected, silent, poor, obscure, laborious." [87] Manual work was also an integral part of this life, and that is what attracted him to the Trappists. "Work has an important place here and that pleases me. Not that I like work, but it is poverty's companion. It is the imitation of Our Lord. It is work that makes Trappist life into a Nazareth."[88] He wrote to his sister, who had asked for details about his life:

During autumn, our work consisted in harvesting the vines and clearing the fields. During winter we sawed wood and in the springtime we hoed around

---

86. Meditation, Nazareth, July 25, 1898.
87. Meditation, Nazareth, July 19, 1898.
88. Letter to Fr. Eugene, June 8, 1892.

the vines. In the summer we brought in the hay and harvest. Two days ago we finished harvesting. It's peasants' work, an occupation that is infinitely beneficial to the soul, for while it occupies the body, it leaves the soul free to pray and meditate.[89]

Even though Charles's understanding of Nazareth would go through different phases, the heart of it would always be an interior life with God. "To be alone in the universe with God is the first lesson Fr. Polycarpe gave me and I bless him for this lesson."[90] He wrote to a Trappist friend preparing for ordination:

The soul will produce fruit to the exact measure that the interior man has taken shape. If his interior life is absent, there may be plenty of zeal, good intentions, and hard work but there will be no fruit. It's a spring that wants to channel sanctity to others, but is incapable since it contains none. We can only give what we are, and it's in solitude, in a life alone with God alone, in a deep recollection of the soul that has forgotten the created order so as to live united to God alone, that God gives Himself entirely to the one who gives himself entirely to Him.[91]

Later on, even if he was trekking through the Sahara, he could write, "Whether I am walking or in my hermitage makes little difference because my heart and my eyes remain above. They are in an immense peace, fixed on our heavenly abode."[92] The little house of Nazareth had

---

89. Letter to Marie de Blic, July 3, 1891.
90. Letter to Fr. Eugene, June 8, 1892 (Dom Polycarpe, his novice master, is quoting St. Teresa of Avila).
91. Letter to Fr. Jerome, May 19, 1898.
92. Letter to Henri de Castries, July 15, 1904.

become his *heavenly abode* and he could carry it with him wherever he went. Entering that house gave him a joy no one could take away. The same holds true for us. No building or way of life can ever introduce us into God's presence if we have not first discovered that *little house within*.

Nazareth: A poor house

Life as a Trappist offered Charles the intimacy he desired with Jesus, but very quickly he felt a discrepancy between the poverty endured by the Holy Family and the kind of poverty a monastic setting offered him. He wrote to Fr. Huvelin: "You hope that I have enough poverty . . . No, we are poor in the eyes of rich people but we aren't poor as Our Lord was."[93] He wrote to his cousin: "Eight days ago I was sent to attend the wake of a poor local Catholic who had died in the next village: what a difference between his house and our buildings. I long for Nazareth."[94]

He appreciated the silence offered to him by a monastery, but the structured life which guaranteed that silence was in contradiction with his conception of Nazareth. He felt called to go somewhere else, somewhere *lower*.

On leaving the Trappists, he made private vows in the presence of his confessor: a vow of perpetual chastity and a vow "never to have in my possession nor at my disposal more than a poor workman can have."[95] People have often commented on the fact that brother Charles's spiritual trajectory is reflected in the way he dressed. When he left the Trappists to go to Nazareth he made himself a tunic out of a Trappist habit, gathering it at the waist with a rosary of big beads. On his head

---

93. Letter to Fr. Huvelin, November 5, 1890.
94. Letter to Marie de Bondy, April 10, 1894.
95. *In the Footsteps of Jesus of Nazareth*, p. 59.

he had a white woollen cap which he had sewn together with some string, and around which he rolled a strip of fabric in the form of a turban. He reckoned that his outfit "sang the beautiful poem of divine abjection,"[96] but the Poor Clare nuns declared that it only made him look pathetic and ridiculous!

Nazareth: Where you learn to be a brother

Being a servant for the Poor Clares in Nazareth allowed brother Charles to reconcile the two dimensions of Nazareth he had discovered. He had both a setting that favored silent prayer and a *low-ranking job* which provided him with *abjection*. Adopting the language of *Rerum Novarum* (1891), he wished to be the image of the divine *worker* of Nazareth. The sisters asked him to sweep up and do various errands. He was still a bit high with his newfound happiness when he said to Jesus, "You lived for thirty years as a poor workman in this town of Nazareth whose ground I am blessed to tread and where I have the unutterable, blessed, profound, and inexpressible joy of picking up manure off the streets."[97] He had offered to help the sister who did the garden by picking up the manure along the road in the early morning. Most of his plans for manual work remained just plans—according to the sisters he didn't even know how to plant ordinary lettuce! Nonetheless, he reminded them of St. Francis and they venerated their servant-hermit who, outside of serving Mass and going to the post office, spent most of his time drawing holy pictures and writing up his rules and meditations.

---

96.   Letter to Fr. Huvelin, October 15, 1898.
97.   Retreat in Nazareth, November 5-15, 1897.

The three and a half years spent at the Poor Clares were like a second novitiate, a time when his deep spiritual personality took shape. During his first pilgrimage to Nazareth brother Charles had seen the Incarnation as an expression of God's humility. But living in Nazareth helped him discover that it was more than that. If God had emptied himself, it was in order to make himself close to people. "This love is active and alive. It is deep. It made God cover at a single leap the distance separating the finite from the infinite. It made Him choose an unprecedented means for our salvation: the Incarnation."[98] He gradually discovered the *apostolic dimension of Nazareth.* It began to take on more importance alongside his meditation on Matthew 25:31-46, where the Son of Man identified himself with the *least of his brothers and sisters.* This challenged him. Friendship with Jesus was intimate but not closed in on itself. Where was he with regard to Jesus' presence in the *least*? Imitating Christ in depth required that he lead his Nazareth life, "not where the ground is most hallowed but where souls are in the greatest need." [99]He too needed to cover the distance that separated him from the poor, the lame, the blind . . .

Nazareth: Where your life is most useful for your neighbor

Brother Charles dreamed of returning to Morocco, which he had explored as a young man. It seemed the place where "souls were in the greatest need." But Morocco remained closed. He settled as closely as possible on the Algerian side of the border in a large oasis called Beni

---

98. Meditation on Luke 1:38 during a retreat in Ephrem, March 14, 1898.
99. Letter to Msgr. Caron, April 8, 1905.

Abbès. Whereas before he had put the accent on imitating the *divine workman* in Nazareth, now he sought to be a *universal brother*. After three and a half years in a hermitage, his naïve generosity quickly drove him at an unsustainable rhythm of life. Having built his *Fraternity*, he wrote to Dom Martin, the abbot of Our Lady of the Snows:

> Guests, poor people, slaves, visitors—they don't leave me a minute's peace. I'm the only one, with all the work of the monastery to do. I finished the little guest house on the 15th and since then every day we've had guests to lodge and to feed morning and evening. The place hasn't been empty once. There are as many as eleven a night, not counting an old cripple who lives there permanently. I have 60 to 100 visitors a day, quite often if not always.[100]

Once again, one can't help but smile on reading the letters he wrote to Fr. Huvelin, complaining of sleeping during his night vigils. "I'm ashamed and upset that I am so overcome by sleep. It takes up more of my life than I want it to. I don't have time for it, but it just takes over."[101] With what wisdom Fr. Huvelin wrote: "Be humble and patient with yourself, less concerned with minimizing your need for sleep than with decreasing the anxiety and restlessness that torment you with a constant feeling of dissatisfaction."[102]

Two years later General Laperrine invited him to take part in a convoy heading for the south Sahara among the Tuareg people, who were even more destitute than those of Beni Abbès. The goal of the expedition was a

---

100. Letter to Dom Martin, February 7, 1902.
101. Letter to Fr. Huvelin, December 15, 1902.
102. Letter from Fr. Huvelin, April 18, 1899.

fraternization tour, but brother Charles very quickly considered settling there. At a crossroads near Tit he saw two locations that lent themselves to an establishment. He could easily make a chapel and some rooms out of the boulders and grottos beside the wadi. But he also noticed a *gara* (rocky outcrop) on which there was just enough room to place an oratory measuring less than five by seven feet!

Sketch by Charles de Foucauld, May 26, 1904: Tit, at the foot of the gara

He debated within himself. Next to the wadi it would be easy to build and it would cost little. But the proximity of the track meant that he might be exposing himself to a lot of visitors. Building on top of the *gara* would require much work but have the advantage of discouraging visitors and granting him solitude with God. After weighing the pros and cons he prayed: "May the Beloved deign to tell me which of the two places he wants for me today." Given the number of guests he was receiving in Beni Abbès, it was hardly surprising that he felt attracted by the *gara*! But he heard an inner voice:

> Today and in the future, if you can, settle me in the first place, among the boulders that resemble those of Bethlehem and Nazareth. There you will have the perfection both of imitating me and that of charity; as for recollection, it's love that must recollect you

interiorly in me and not distancing yourself from my children: *See me in them, and like me in Nazareth, live close to them, lost in God.*[103]

In just a few words, the Beloved gave him the key that would guide the rest of his journey: his life wasn't a matter of reconciling prayer and contemplation on the one hand with activities and ministry on the other. He was called to a new form of religious life that drew its inspiration directly from the Incarnation: a contemplative life in the fullest sense of the word, but one that deepened through daily contact with human reality.

Nazareth: Where you learn to listen

When he arrived in Tamanrasset, brother Charles was not given a warm welcome. Although the Tuareg leader gave him permission to settle there, he had arrived in the company of the French army. He was shown a place on the other side of the wadi from the village, where he could build his house. He would need to break the ice. But in order to do that, he would first need to learn the language.

Right from the beginning of his tours among the Tuareg, brother Charles had begun to study their language. He always walked beside the interpreter who accompanied the convoy. By the time he settled in Tamanrasset he had prepared a Tuareg version of the four Gospels. After settling, it did not take him long to realize that his translation was very poor. The interpreter was familiar with a Tuareg dialect other than that spoken in the Hoggar. How, then, could he set about truly learning the local language? He appealed for help to his friend Adolphe Motylinski. Motylinski's arrival in Tamanrasset marked

---

103. Beni Abbès notebook, May 26, 1904.

an important turning point in brother Charles's thinking. He made Charles understand that to learn a language, you don't start by translating what you want to say, but by listening. Tuareg people readily expressed themselves in poems sung at courtly celebrations around the campfire, so Charles and Motylinski started a collection of these songs, which would become the basis for their study of Tamahaq, the Tuareg language.

In an article printed while brother Charles was still alive, General Laperrine wrote:

> It's a great boon for Father de Foucauld whenever he can get a hold of a few old ladies of the high Tuareg nobility, because they are the ones who are the most familiar with traditions, legends, genealogies, poetry, etc. Nothing is so funny as to see him, pencil in hand, enthroned amidst a gathering of old ladies seated on the ground around him, chatting as they sip their tea and smoke their pipes.[104]

The more he got to know the Tuareg, the more he realized how much French occupation threatened their culture. As he prepared his collection of their poems, he wrote to an editor: "It is imperative that this work be done soon. Now there's a moratorium on raiding and pillaging. Peace is compulsory and that results in poverty. There are no more intrepid heroes to sing about, nothing to lighten their hearts, no more dazzling outfits for the evening *ahâl*."[105]

Motylinski's premature death in March 1907 left Charles alone before an enormous undertaking that had only barely begun. The compilation of a dictionary, which would in fact be an encyclopedia of Tuareg life, would oc-

---

104. Henri Laperrine, "The Stages in the Conversion of a Houzard," *Revue de Cavalerie*, October 1913.

105. Letter to René Basset, May 29, 1908.

cupy the rest of his life. He finished his translation of their poems just three days before his death. In 1911 he noted his daily timetable:

IESUS ± CARITAS	Cor Jesu sacratissimum adveniat regnum tuum
3:30-6:00	Prayer
3:30-4:00	Angelus, Veni Creator, Matins, Lauds.
4:00-5:00	Preparation for Mass, Mass, Thanksgiving.
5:00-6:00	Housekeeping, frustulum; Prime, Terce, Sext, None, Holy Gospel and written meditation; Elevations; Imitation.
6:00-11:30	Work
11:30-12:30	Prayer and dinner: Angelus, Veni Creator; examen; dinner.
12:30-6:00	Work
6:00-8:00	Prayer and collation
6:00-7:00	Vespers; Rosary.
7:00-8:00	Collation; housekeeping; Compline; Consecration to the Sacred Heart; Angelus, Veni Creator; examen.

The biggest portion of his time was taken by *work*, which meant work on his dictionary and poetry anthology. He first embarked on this task because he saw it as an indispensable instrument for those who would later come to evangelize the Tuareg. But little by little he became fascinated with what he was discovering. The final version of his dictionary far surpassed what a missionary might need! It is a capacity that has much in common with contemplation.

Nazareth in all its simplicity and breadth

Brother Charles arrived in Tamanrasset on July 22, 1907, the feast of St. Mary Magdalene. In his notebook he jotted down what he imagined his beloved *patroness of the desert*[106] would want to tell him regarding his new settlement. She encouraged him to be less rigid!

> In everything and for everything, take the life of Nazareth as your object, until it becomes really possible to lead a life completely as Little Brothers and Little Sisters in a cloistered Nazareth. Let Nazareth be your model, in all its simplicity and breadth, using your Rule as a handbook of guidelines which will sometimes help you find the way to the life of Nazareth. . . . Use the Rule of the Little Brothers to help you lead this life as you would a holy book; take your distance from it resolutely in all that doesn't help you to a perfect imitation of this life. . . . Your Nazareth life can be lead anywhere; lead it where it is the most useful for your neighbor.[107]

Knowing his attachment to his rule, it is astounding to hear him say to himself that it can sometimes hinder his imitation of the life of Nazareth and that he must take a distance from it! Those he later called his *Muslim parishioners*[108] would have a great role in helping him discover what that involved.

---

106. Brother Charles was very fond of a French Provençal legend which held that St. Mary Magdalene had finished her days as a hermit in a grotto (la Sainte Baume) not far from Marseilles.
107. Tamanrasset notebook, July 22, 1905.
108. Expression he uses in a letter to Marie de Bondy, September 4, 1912.

During his final years, living Nazareth *in its simplicity and breadth* meant being in a relationship with his neighbors where he wasn't just on the giving end. On returning from his first trip back to France he wrote to a friend: "These first days back are anything but days of solitude; I was given an affectionate welcome by the Tuareg, and it touched me. They are constantly here."[109]

On the eve of the synod on the family in October 2015, Pope Francis said:

> Charles de Foucauld, perhaps like few others, grasped the import of the spirituality which radiates from Nazareth. . . . Attracted by the life of a hermit, he came to understand that we do not grow in the love of God by avoiding the entanglement of human relations. For in loving others, we learn to love God; in stooping down to help our neighbour, we are lifted up to God. Through his fraternal closeness and his solidarity with the poor and the abandoned, he came to understand that it is they who evangelize us, they who help us to grow in humanity.[110]

This way of understanding Nazareth echoes what the Gospels tells us about Jesus. He spent the first thirty years of his life listening to the people of his village, putting all his divine power and generosity into becoming a man from Nazareth, into speaking like the people of his hometown. When he started preaching the Kingdom of God, he did it using their language and their actions. Their lives were his teaching material: the sower who went out to his field, the woman who swept her house

---

109. Letter to Henri de Castries, May 16, 1911.
110. "Address of His Holiness Pope Francis at the Prayer Vigil in Preparation for the XIV Ordinary General Assembly of the Synod of Bishops," October 3, 2015, accessed online.

in search of lost money, the drama of a father who saw his son leave for the big city where he squandered his money in bad company. His listeners were amazed that he had recognized the Kingdom in their lives. This dialogue needs to be pursued with men and women today. People need those who can recognize and name the presence of the Kingdom in their lives.

There is a lapse of thirty years from brother Charles's conversion in 1886 until his death in 1916. According to St. Luke, this is how long Jesus spent in Nazareth. Charles's spiritual itinerary, which would move from separation to proximity, is steeped in Nazareth. In learning to become close to people, he never forgot his starting point, which was a life lived for God alone. Several months before his death he wrote a letter where he confessed that all he had really learned in life was how to "pray in solitude, keep silence, live with books and at most, chat intimately one-on-one with poor people."[111] Chatting one-on-one with the poor went hand in hand with solitary prayer. Meeting God always makes us closer to each human being, especially those in greater need of respect and appreciation.

When brother Charles was going through his vocational crisis as a Trappist, Fr. Huvelin had written to him: "Nazareth is a house that you build in your heart, or better still, it's a house that you allow the hands of Jesus, the child so meek and humble of heart, to build inside of you."[112] Even if Nazareth is a little house, it has room for a lot of people!

---

111. Letter to Fr. Voillard, June 11, 1916.
112. Letter from Fr. Huvelin, August 2, 1896.

5

The Universal Brother

"It's first about being a brother, before thinking about being universal." (Brother Antoine Chatelard)

Not finding among the Trappists the "humble life of Nazareth" to which he felt called, Charles began to wonder if he shouldn't start something new. While readily admitting that he did not have the makings of a founder, in 1893, only three years after joining the Trappists, he drafted a rule for the congregation of his dreams, which he called the *Little Brothers of Jesus.*

In the first article, he wrote, "Ardently desiring to bear His beloved name, we have dared to take it, adding those of *Little* and *Brothers,* in memory of His oft-repeated recommendation to be little and His counsel to call each other brothers."[113] He sent his rule to Fr. Huvelin, who was alarmed on reading it. "The rule is impossible, and it contains everything but discretion. I am broken-hearted."[114] He gave Charles permission to express his doubts regarding his vocation as a Trappist but begged him to forgo the idea of becoming a founder.

Having settled next to the Poor Clare Sisters in Nazareth, brother Charles hoped that he had found his *everlasting home.* Yet, in spite of Fr. Huvelin's reservations, the desire to found kept coming back. He wanted to belong to something. During his third year in Nazareth he drew up a

---

113. Rule for the Union of Brothers and Sisters of the Sacred Heart, Article I. Found in *Charles de Foucauld, Règlements et Directoire*, Nouvelle Cité, p. 28.
114. Bazin, p. 99.

new rule for a congregation that now bore the name of *The Hermits of the Sacred Heart of Jesus.* He imagined their way of life based on what he himself was living.

Having finished his rule, brother Charles decided to present it to the Latin Patriarch of Jerusalem for approval, so that he could wear the habit, call himself a Hermit of the Sacred Heart, and be ordained to the priesthood. He set off from Nazareth to Jerusalem on foot. One senses that his first biographer, René Bazin, took pleasure in describing his arrival at the patriarchate:

> In what a dress and in how pitiable a condition!
> . . . On the way his sandals must have given out on the road; he had replaced them by mere bits of wood strapped together. Bands of thick paper tied up with string hid the holes in his breeches, torn at both knees. . . . His Beatitude quickly sent him away, imagining that he was dealing with one of those visionary cranks who are not uncommon in the Middle East—or elsewhere.[115]

He returned to France therefore and spent a year at Our Lady of the Snows, where the Trappists agreed to prepare him for ordination. During that time, he received many insights into his special vocation, and it would mark a turning point. His initial plan had been to return to the Holy Land after ordination but, as he explained in a letter, "My retreats before being ordained to the diaconate and to the priesthood showed me that I ought to lead the life of Nazareth, which is my vocation, not in the Holy Land I love so well but among the people whose souls were most sick, the sheep who were most forsaken." [116]

---

115. Ibid., p. 133.
116. Letter to Msgr. Caron, April 8, 1905.

The apostolic dimension of Nazareth was coming to the fore and finding its expression in the word *brother*. He went back to his rule, scratching out the word *hermit* and replacing it with stickers that read *little brother*. The brothers were to live in *fraternities*. "Their fraternities dedicated to the SACRED HEART OF JESUS must, like Jesus, radiate over the earth and *set it ablaze*."[117]

This intuition marked the first communities born of his spirituality, who called themselves *fraternities*. The word *congregation* put the accent on a gathering of members, whereas *fraternity* highlighted a quality of relationship among community members which extended to people outside the group.

Years later, as he tried to organize a confraternity for the evangelization of the colonies, brother Charles wrote a letter to a layman in Lyons, Joseph Hours, in which he summarized his thoughts regarding mission:

> Every Christian must be an apostle. This is not a counsel; it is a commandment, the commandment of charity. But be an apostle in what way? . . . Above all, apostles must see every human being as their brother or sister: "You are all brothers and sisters since you have only one Father, and he is in heaven." They must see in every human being a child of God.[118]

The apostolate consisted in recognizing a brother or sister in the other person and behaving accordingly.

---

117. Rule for the Union of Brothers and Sisters of the Sacred Heart, Article XXXVII.
118. Letter to J. Hours, May 3, 1912.

Fraternity at the heart of the Bible

My years of sharing brother Charles with others have taught me that his intuitions strike a deeper chord when set in resonance with Scripture. The importance he attributes to fraternity echoes a central biblical theme.

The Book of Genesis presents humanity as being born of the same parents. It follows that living together as brothers and sisters is fundamental to the human vocation. But too often, that vocation is betrayed. After humanity's expulsion from Paradise, the first story the Bible narrates in this real world involves a deadly conflict between brothers:

> Now Adam knew Eve his wife, and she conceived and bore Cain, saying, "I have gotten a man with the help of the Lord." And again, she bore his brother Abel. Now Abel was a keeper of sheep, and Cain a tiller of the ground. In the course of time Cain brought to the Lord an offering of the fruit of the ground, and Abel brought of the firstlings of his flock and of their fat portions. And the Lord had regard for Abel and his offering, but for Cain and his offering he had no regard. So Cain was very angry, and his countenance fell.[119]

The older son can be credited with having been the first to think of offering a sacrifice to the Lord. His younger brother follows suit and whereas God looks with favor on his offering, he does not look with favor on that of the older son. Is God unfair? Once again, the Bible speaks to us through its omissions. We are given no reason for God's preference. The author wants to provoke us. What he describes, in fact, corresponds to our experience. Life

---

119. Genesis 4:1-5

is not fair. We always have an Abel at our side, someone who has more—who is more talented, more beautiful, better loved! Why is one person born healthy and another crippled? Why is one person born where there is peace, another where there is war?

Cain's story isn't tragic, but he's going to make it into a tragedy. Abel is preferred, but Cain isn't rejected. In the narrative God never speaks with Abel, only with Cain. But like his parents, Cain pays no attention to what he has. He sees only what he doesn't have. And having *less* is going to gnaw away at his heart.

According to the Bible, the great human challenge is to live peacefully with those whom we think have *more* than ourselves. God warns Cain, "Sin is couching at the door; its desire is for you, but you must master it." He reminds Cain of his vocation, for like his parents he has been granted dominion over the animals. But like his parents, Cain allows himself to be mastered by an animal. Swallowed by the beast that couched at his door, he becomes beastly towards his brother and spills his blood— the blood which made them brothers.

God then asks Cain, "Where is Abel your brother?" It recalls his question to Adam, "Where are you?" The two questions suggest that standing before God involves standing beside one's brother or sister. Cain brazenly replies, "Am I my brother's keeper?" When he leaves the Lord's presence he expresses no repentance. His sin remains unresolved. The writer suggests that we live in a world where many things are unresolved.[120]

The chapters that follow describe humanity's slide into ever-greater violence, and God's heart grieves. He no longer recognizes his world. His initial response to violence will be violent, and that's often what we would like him to do! He sends the flood. But afterward God

---

120. See Genesis 4:6-16.

repents. His attachment to humanity is so strong that he prefers to have human beings as they are rather than no human beings at all. But then he will have to intervene once again, for what he created, he must now save. It is not just individuals that need saving; if God wants to put an end to violence, it is the bond between human beings that needs saving.

A bond that only the Father can mend

In his book *Jesus of Nazareth*, Joseph Ratzinger begins his commentary on the parable of the prodigal son with the following:

> The theme of the two brothers runs through the entire Old Testament. Beginning with Cain and Abel, it continues down through Ishmael and Isaac to Esau and Jacob, only to be reflected once more in a modified form in the behavior of the eleven sons of Jacob toward Joseph. The history of those chosen by God is governed by a remarkable dialectic between pairs of brothers and it remains an unresolved question in the Old Testament.[121]

The First Book of Kings narrates the political schism between the twelve tribes (who, as children of Israel, are brothers) and the religious schism that ensued. It resulted in the deportation of the northern tribes to Assyria where they were assimilated and disappeared. Only Judah remained. In calling the twelve apostles, starting with two sets of brothers, Jesus was indicating his intention of leading Israel's vocation to fulfillment. He did not come

---

121. Joseph Ratzinger, *Jesus of Nazareth*, New York: Doubleday, 2007, p. 203.

to found a new religion but to repair the broken bonds within humanity.

In the parable of the prodigal son,[122] the elder son refuses to enter the house to take part in a banquet in honor of his younger brother. When the father comes out to plead with him, the bitterness that has been building up for years bursts out. "All these years I have slaved for you and never once disobeyed any orders of yours, yet you never offered me so much as a kid for me to celebrate with my friends. But for this son of yours, when he comes back after swallowing up your property—he and his loose women—you kill the calf we had been fattening."

His anger is focused on the fatted calf, which is mentioned three times. In fact, it's the key to his story. The fatted calf is a *golden calf*, synonymous with the idolatry that lurks behind any absence of brotherhood. He who refuses his brother does not know God. The father tries to rekindle a sense of brotherhood in him by reminding him of his identity: "My son, you are with me always and all I have is yours." We don't know how the story ends. Does he go into the banquet? His decision will depend on his capacity and willingness to take in his father's words.

In his book *A Messiah named Joseph*, Rabbi Eisenberg writes:

> How can people become brothers—or rather, since they already are brothers—how can they avoid becoming enemies? History has clearly demonstrated that the fact of being brothers has never been sufficient reason to prevent conflicts from erupting. Hence, a new dimension needs to be introduced into human relationships. And that, I think, is the purpose and justification of religion: not to content ourselves with saying, "we are all brothers," but to affirm with

---

122. See Luke 15:11-32

the prophet: "Do we not all have the same father?"
Only the awareness of a shared love for God seems
capable of awakening a harmonious, conflict-free
sense of fraternity.[123]

Brother Charles did not want to be a brother who
just sat back waiting for his younger prodigal brother to
show up. Knowing his Father's heart, he set off to look
for him in his far-away country. That's what brought
him to the desert.

In Beni Abbès brother Charles called his establishment the *Fraternity of the Sacred Heart of Jesus*. He drew
his inspiration from the *zaouïas* (seats of Muslim confra-
ternities), encountered during his exploration in Morocco.
These served as places of prayer and hospitality for trav-
elers. He wanted his establishment to be comprehensible
to local people. But his *zaouïa* had an important difference, namely, the presence of the Blessed Sacrament. The
way he arranged his chapel said a lot about his spirituality. It was the first time he had a place of his own and he
arranged it in such a way that it expressed what was in his
heart. He wrote to his cousin:

> You have asked me for a description of the chapel.
> . . . The chapel dedicated to the Sacred Heart of
> Jesus is called the "Chapel of the Fraternity of the
> Sacred Heart of Jesus." My little abode is called
> "The Fraternity of the Sacred Heart of Jesus." . . .
> I want all the people here, be they Christian, Muslim,
> Jewish, or whatever, to look on me as their brother, the
> universal brother. They are starting to call my house
> "the fraternity" (the *Khaoua* in Arabic) and that gives
> me pleasure. . . . Above the altar there's a life-sized

---

123. Josy Eisenberg and Benno Gross, *Un Messie nommé Joseph,*
Paris: Albin Michel, 1983, p. 121.

picture of the Sacred Heart, standing. It's the penitent Sacred Heart,[124] stretching out His arms to welcome, call and embrace all people, giving Himself for them and offering them His heart. It stretches from the top of the Tabernacle to the ceiling, covering the whole back wall. It's exactly the same width as the altar. I'm the one who drew and painted the Sacred Heart. When I don't have a picture I like, I make one myself, counting on people's indulgence![125]

He dressed in the same way as the picture in his chapel, because he wanted to be the instrument of a fraternity that had its source in the heart of Jesus.

From the particular to the universal

If brother Charles attached such importance to the words *brother* and *fraternity,* one can suppose that his family experience was in the background. After he left for the Trappists, Marie de Bondy wrote to Father Eugene:

> God asked us for a great sacrifice when he took Charles away. To me, he was like a younger brother. For many years he shared all our trials with absolute devotion and a most faithful affection. He left a great emptiness. The better you know him, the more you will understand my sadness, which, however, is not a complaint.[126]

---

124. A reference to the representation of the Sacred Heart in the Basilica of the Sacré Cœur in Paris, which was built to fulfill a national vow made in penitence for the blood shed during the French Revolution.
125. Letter to Marie de Bondy, January 7, 1902.
126. Marie de Bondy to Fr. Eugene, January 23, 1890.

Even though it broke his heart to leave his family, he himself said, "convent life doesn't shrivel up your heart, but enlarges it."[127] It would make him capable of extending the bonds of tenderness and affection he had experienced in his family to all those he met, especially the poorest.

In the Rule for the Little Brothers, the chapter on charity said:

> May their universal and brotherly charity shine like a beacon for all around. Let none of those, near or far, sinner or infidel,[128] be unaware that they are universal friends, universal brothers who spend their life praying for everyone without exception and doing them good. Their fraternity is a port, a refuge where all people, especially the poor and destitute, are always fraternally invited, desired, and welcomed.[129]

It was easy to write those lines in the solitude of his hermitage in Nazareth, but not so easy to live them on the front lines of French colonial expansion in the Algerian Sahara, ravaged by conflicts of every kind. Beni Abbès came under French occupation in March 1901 and brother Charles arrived seven months later on October 28. Two villages were nestled among seven thousand palm trees. One was Berber (with one thousand inhabitants) and the other Arab (with seven hundred inhabitants), including a large number of slaves of sub-Saharan origin in both villages. The garrison was built on the cliff that overlooked the villages. It housed eight hundred soldiers, only two hundred of whom were French, the rest being Algerians

---

127. Letter to Gabriel Tourdes, May 11, 1891.
128. Way of designating non-Christians at the time.
129. Article XXX

serving in the occupying army. The population also included sixty Jews and two Spanish merchants. Brother Antoine Chatelard writes:

> Being a universal brother is first about being a brother, before thinking about being universal. When [Charles] wrote his Rule in Nazareth, he could only imagine "the poor, the rich, sinners and infidels." . . . In Beni-Abbès, these were real flesh-and-blood people coming and knocking at his door. Each day his "without exception" took on a different and concrete face. Universal love doesn't exist outside of the particular. It means loving that person who is right in front of me, not loving the idea of someone I have never set eyes on.[130]

Brother Charles wanted to be a *universal brother*. By looking at his particular relationships, we can understand what that meant.

Redeeming slaves

In Beni Abbès his *brotherly welcome*, which included food, earned him from sixty to one hundred visitors per day. Many of these visitors were children. Kidnapped in French Sudan, they had later been sold in the marketplace as slaves. Despite France's official position, the military commanders who first arrived in Beni Abbès decided against abolishing slavery, in order to obtain the peaceful submission of both villages. Brother Charles was irate. He asked the Trappists and White Fathers to stir up public opinion back in France, writing:

---

130. Antoine Chatelard, *Universal Fraternity in the Life of Charles de Foucauld,* Little Brothers of Jesus Document.

Woe to you hypocrites, who print on your stamps and all around, Liberty, Equality, Fraternity, Human Rights, while you clamp iron fetters on slaves. You condemn people who counterfeit banknotes to the galleys while you allow children to be stolen from their parents and publicly sold. You punish the theft of a chicken while you permit the theft of a man.[131]

The White Fathers asked him to control his zeal, since it threatened their missions and imperiled the little relief they could offer. They were an institution, and their relationship with the French Republic was under much greater strain than that of brother Charles, who was acting as an individual. Charles complied but answered his apostolic prefect[132]:

I will obey to the letter the directives you've given me. The reasons you have been good enough to express to me so affectionately, which carry such weight because they come from you, still do not leave me without regret . . . that the representatives of Jesus are content to defend "in whispers" (and not from the rooftops) a cause which is after all one of justice and charity.[133]

He did, however, redeem some slaves, which was one of the reasons he had so many people coming to his door. This led to conflicts with the slave owners. Among the children he redeemed was three-year-old Salême, whom he christened Abd-Jesu. Marie de Bondy agreed to be his godmother and received regular updates:

---

131. Letter to Dom Martin, February 7, 1902.
132. The Apostolic Prefecture of the North Sahara had been entrusted to the White Fathers.
133. Letter to Msgr. Guérin, September 17, 1902.

September 12, 1902

Your godson is of great service to me. Each morning he serves my Mass to the best of his ability, while nibbling on his breakfast. Thanks to him I can celebrate Mass before the troops get up,[134] before daybreak and all the bustle. It's a real grace to have some recollection at that time.

October 18, 1902

Nothing new here. Abd-Jesu is holding my hand and playing with it while I write to you with the other one. He is well, and he is a good boy. He responds to the litany and sings the Tantum Ergo and Veni Creator with all his heart.

November 29, 1902

Pardon my handwriting. It is partly my fault, partly due to the cold, but mostly due to your godson who, after settling on my knees, won't sit still for a second. He sings and dances at the same time, and it seems to me that it is better to try your patience and your eyesight than to chase this poor little one away from his perch. His early childhood has not been easy and living under JESUS' roof should be a comfort. He is still very good, very healthy, we continue to live in community: he, Paul, and myself.[135]

---

134. Liturgical norms of the day did not permit the celebration of Mass alone.

135. *Bulletin des Amitiés Charles de Foucauld*, October 2007, no. 168.

Brother Charles lived almost a year in the constant presence of Abd-Jesu. He wrote that there was no one trustworthy with whom he could leave him for even a minute. His letters convey a great tenderness for the child, although one can understand his concern that Abd-Jesu might receive better care than he could provide!

With those in the military

Knowing brother Charles's profound love of solitude and the hectic rhythm of his days in Beni Abbès, one can better imagine how much charity it demanded of him to invite Adjutant Joyeux to spend his evenings at the Fraternity. The desert caused depression in some men and he knew from his own experience how boring life in a garrison could be.

> Dear friend, You told me that you are depressed at night and that your evenings are dull. . . . Will you— if you are allowed to leave the camp, which I do not know—come and spend the evenings regularly with me? We shall make them as long as you like, chatting fraternally of the future, of your children and your plans . . . of what you and those you love more than yourself want and hope for. . . . You will find a brother's heart, if nothing else.
>
> The poor man offers you what he has. What he offers you, above all, is his very tender and brotherly affection, his profound devotion in the Heart of Jesus.
>
> Brother Charles of Jesus[136]

---

136. Bazin, p. 155.

Friendship with his apostolic prefect

Despite tension around the problem of slavery, a deep friendship bound brother Charles to Charles Guérin, the young White Father named apostolic prefect of the Sahara at twenty-nine years of age. They were kindred spirits and he was one of the few people who deeply understood brother Charles. The distances being so huge, Msgr. Guérin visited him in Beni Abbès only once, in June 1903. After five days together, Msgr. Guérin set off, taking Abd-Jesu with him. A few days later Charles sent him a note: "For the first time in many years, *I felt alone* on Monday evening as you disappeared little by little into the night. I understood, I felt that I was a hermit. Then I remembered that I had JESUS and I said, 'JESUS I love you.'"[137] For brother Charles to say that he felt alone on seeing Msgr. Guérin leave speaks volumes about their friendship.

With the Tuareg

As he set off with a military convoy on a pacification tour, brother Charles was keenly aware of the ambiguity of his situation. He wrote to Msgr. Guérin:

> The natives receive us well. It is not sincere: they yield to necessity. How long will it be before they really feel what they now pretend to? . . . Will they know how to distinguish soldiers from priests, to see in us God's servants, ministers of peace and charity, universal brothers? I do not know. If I do my duty, Jesus will pour down abundant graces, and they will understand.[138]

---

137. Letter to Msgr. Guérin, June 3, 1903.
138. Letter to Msgr. Guérin, July 4, 1904.

One cannot evangelize a people who have been crushed. Brother Charles responded to the destitution he encountered in Tamanrasset in the many little ways he could. His brick molds were in constant demand, allowing people to replace their *zribas*[139] with sturdy houses. One can also think of his efforts to teach the people knitting! During his third and longest trip to France, in the company of a young Tuareg called Oûksem, he thought of his neighbors who lacked warm clothing and asked his cousin to teach him how to knit. Once they were back he wrote to her:

> Knitting and crochet are catching on wonderfully. Everyone has started; the women do both. Quite a few young people crochet themselves vests. But we no longer have crochet hooks, wool, or cotton. If you could send me some . . . and also have Vilmorin send me some cotton seed. It would be of great service to those here. . . . All of these things are spiritually useful, because everything goes together.[140]

It is poignant to imagine the former officer learning to knit, even if Oûksem was to later write to brother Charles's nephew in broken French, "Knitting Oûksem gazelle, knitting Marabout slug."

There were not just little actions. Foremost among the bigger things was brother Charles's linguistic efforts to know and preserve the Tuareg culture. He also frequently served as a paramedic among his entourage. He learned a lot in the company of military doctors and had a notebook where he recorded various diseases and remedies. During the great famine of 1907-1908 he prepared meals once a day for the village children. He also served as a spokesman

---

139. Reed huts
140. Letter to Marie de Bondy, April 16, 1915.

for the Tuareg in some of their dealings with the French authorities. The army demanded that the Tuareg provide them with camels and guides. Brother Charles helped the Tuareg write a letter asking for an increase in rental rates for their camels or in the price of their butter, declaring that the authorities' demand for butter was cruel in time of drought, when there wasn't a drop of milk.

His "apostolate of goodness" didn't just mean doing good *to* the Tuareg, but doing it as a *brother*. He used to jot down "things to tell Moussa" (the Tuareg chief). For example, Charles recommended that he "always furnish thoroughly good men as guides, because often all the other Tuareg get judged by them." He also recommended, "Never ask the Captain for sugar, tea, or anything; bring what is necessary, and if you lack anything, put up with it. If you ask, you get what you want but at the same time you obtain what you don't wish for—contempt."[141] In both cases, that is advice coming from a brother—he wants the Tuareg to be respected.

Moussa was sensitive to this attitude. In January 1914 he wrote to Charles from Adrar—about five hundred miles from Tamanrasset—where he had come with his men and camels in search of better pastures during a time of drought. There were frequent skirmishes with Moroccan raiders.

It's me. Moussa, amenokal of the Hoggar. I say: I send many, many greetings to my friend and companion the marabout, servant of Jesus. God be praised for your health! We miss you a lot. I saw your young Oûksem, he gave us your news, thank you very much! I wrote you a letter through the lieutenant in Boughessa. He will pass it on to you. We are well if you are well. Greetings from Tedawit, Akhamouk,

---

141. Bazin, p. 244.

Litni, from everybody and from Rakhma. . . . Don't neglect me! I ask you one thing: pray for me a lot. Greetings! No more paper.[142]

Written on the back of an envelope in *tifinagh* (Tuareg characters) the letter was sent straight to the marabout, bypassing the French administration. One cannot doubt Moussa's sincerity.

Friendship rather than conversions

Brother Charles was impressed by the story of Tarichat, a Tuareg woman who saved a *tirailleur* (native infantryman) serving in the French army. He wrote in his notebook, "Is this soul not ready for the Gospel?"[143] He expressed his longing to evangelize them in a letter to Msgr. Guérin. "I think a great, great deal about the Tuareg, who deserve our special attention, both because they are of a lively, robust, intelligent nature and because they are more open than others and easier to transform. They have not been deeply Islamized."[144] Tuareg were Berbers, from a pre-Islamic culture, and their geographical isolation meant that many were ignorant regarding the content of their faith. The occupiers' religion, however, held no attraction for them, and brother Charles would quickly realize this. Their re-Islamization took place during his lifetime. Instead of discouraging him, it would help him explore more deeply his own form of apostolate.

One senses his great admiration for Islam at the time of his Moroccan adventure, but his re-conversion to Ca-

---

142. *Lettres au Marabout*, ed. Lionel Galand, Paris: Éditions Belins, 1999, p. 162.
143. Beni Abbès notebook, June 21, 1903.
144. Letter to Msgr. Guérin, June 1, 1908.

tholicism made him very critical of Islam. Today we might find him a bit narrow minded. In 1901 he wrote to a friend, "Islam is very seductive. It seduced me greatly. But the Catholic faith is true. It's easy to prove and consequently all the others are false."[145] This didn't mean that he saw nothing good in Islam, but according to him, "Islam falls aside once you are educated. History and philosophy condemn it unequivocally: It cedes its place like night to day."[146] That does not lead him to conclude, however, that *outside of the Church there is no salvation.* Dr. Dautheville, a Protestant army doctor, remembers a meal in his hermitage where he asked brother Charles the following question:

> Do you think that the Tuareg are going to convert and that you will obtain results rewarding you for your sacrifices? "My dear Doctor," he replied, "I am not here to convert the Tuareg all at once but to try to understand them and improve them. I learn their language and study them so that after me other priests will be able to continue my work. I belong to the Church and She has time. She endures, whereas I pass and I don't count. Besides, I want the Tuareg to have their place in Paradise. I am sure that God will open heaven to those who were good and honest without them needing to be Roman Catholic. You are a Protestant, Teissère is an atheist, the Tuareg are Muslim; I am sure God will welcome us all if we deserve it, and I seek to improve the Tuareg so that they deserve Heaven."[147]

This conversation was a distant memory by the time it was written, and brother Charles never explicitly expressed

---

145. Letter to Henri de Castries, July 15, 1901.
146. Letter to Msgr. Caron, June 9, 1908.
147. Sourisseau, *Charles de Foucauld,* p. 481.

that point of view in his writings. But the attitude Dr. Dautheville describes agrees with many stories told about Charles. *Islam* in and of itself occupied very little space in brother Charles's life, compared to the great importance he attached to the *Muslim people* living around him. He was not a theoretician but a hands-on person. Some of his disciples would complete his work by engaging in a dialogue with Islam, but he himself spoke only of *meeting people*, of *living with them*. Moussa gives us an example of what this meant in his letter to René Bazin in 1920.

> You ask me what took place when he was present at the illness of my mother—that is to say, my aunt (Tîhit), my father's sister, at the time of the illness of which she died. The marabout Charles said to her in Tamachek: "Oksâd massinîn" [fear God], and afterwards he left her. She died the next day. We carried the body to the tomb, and he was with us; whilst we were praying for her, he was standing, the colour [of his face] changed on account of her death. He did not pray with us for her. When we placed her in her tomb, he kept standing on the edge, buried her with us, and said to us: "God increase your consolation on the subject of Tîhit! May God give her Paradise in her tomb!"[148]

Robert Hérisson, who also spent some time in Tamanrasset as an army doctor, recalls the following scene:

> One evening, at sunset—that is to say, at one of the hours of Muslim prayer—five or six Tuareg were talking with Father de Foucauld and the amenokal. The latter, his cousin Akhammuk and Aflan, Dassine's husband, rose up, adjusted their blue

---

148. Bazin, p. 304.

lithams on their faces, and prepared to say the prayer. The other Tuareg, indifferent, continued talking. But the Father stopped them sharply: "Well, don't you pray?" he said. They understood, and at once got up to imitate Moussa.[149]

With time brother Charles understood that his vocation wasn't to convert but to prepare the way through building up trust and being close. A fruitful dialogue can only take place within an atmosphere of friendship and respect. An anthropologist who travelled in his company testified:

> He never made a single convert during his fifteen years in the Sahara. We too, his heathen companions, also experienced his discretion. During the many weeks spent together, travelling long distances with a small military convoy, Fr. de Foucauld certainly said his Mass each day, but always alone, with no one other than Paul. . . . We ate our meals together for weeks but the conversation never once took an ecclesiastical turn, never became an attempt to convert us.[150]

Two convictions seemed to guide him: that it was imperative to announce the gospel and that God would receive all people of good will into his Kingdom. How those two truths fit together was God's mystery.

Brother Charles had witnessed the massacre of Armenian Christians in Syria and he was aware of the violent, fanatical streak in certain currents of Islam. He was aware of the danger he faced and wrote to the Trappists several times that should they send him a candidate, the

---

149. Ibid., p. 289.
150. Emile-Felix Gautier, *L'Algérie et la métropole*, Paris: Payot, 1931.

latter should be prepared to "face beheading with great joy for JESUS' sake."[151]

On December 1, 1916, brother Charles was killed by a group of Tuareg from Ajjer (near the Libyan border) who had rallied to the Senussi, a Muslim confraternity that had become radicalized with the European invasion of the Maghreb. The manner of his death is distressingly similar to much that makes the headlines today. But today, just as in brother Charles's time, it would be wrong to place Christians entirely on one side and Muslims on the other. It was during the First World War and the Senussi had been armed by Germany and Turkey. Three Muslim soldiers serving in the French army were killed alongside brother Charles during the raid.

The first one to write a letter of condolence to his family was Moussa:

> To her Ladyship our friend Marie, the sister of Charles our marabout, whom traitors and deceivers, people of Azjer, assassinated, from Tebeul Moussa ag Amastane, *amenokal* of Hoggar.

> Much greeting to our aforesaid friend Marie! As soon as I heard of the death of our friend, your brother Charles, my eyes closed; all is dark to me: I wept and I shed many tears, and I am in great mourning. His death is a great grief to me. . . .

> Say good-day for me to your daughters, your husband, and all your friends, and tell them: Charles the marabout has died not only for you, but for us all. May God have mercy on him, and may we meet him in paradise![152]

151. Letter to Dom Martin, April 24, 1902.
152. Bazin, p. 349.

A flawless figure?

Moussa's letter is certainly a magnificent testimony to the bond that united the two men, but it would be an error to think that brother Charles managed to become a perfect little brother. The severity with which he sometimes expresses himself can jar the reader. He is very harsh in his judgement of Michel, the only companion who ever dared to join him. Within the context of the war he said some terrible things about the Germans. Laperrine remembered feeling a cold shiver run down his back as he heard Charles express how an officer who had abandoned his men during an ambush should be treated. His life, like all of ours, was a long process, a slow *becoming*.

His views regarding colonization require clarification. French troops landed in Algiers in 1830 and the occupation quickly spread to the whole coastal plain. The dominant Church figure at the time was Cardinal Lavigerie, founder of the White Fathers. On arrival in Algiers in 1867 he had declared: "My mission is to make of Algerian soil the cradle of a great, generous, Christian nation, in other words, of another France: to spread around us the true light of a civilization that has the Gospel as its source and Law."[153] Brother Charles would have wholeheartedly endorsed that declaration. But experience would teach him that the great enterprise of *fraternization*, in which he wanted to take part, was not understood that way by the other side. In 1913 he wrote to General Laperrine, who had already been back in France for several years:

I am sad, sad and ashamed to see so much evil going on in a place where it would have been so easy to do so much good. I am ashamed to see France govern its

---

153. Jean-Claude Ceillier, *L'Histoire des Missionaires d'Afrique*, Karthala: Paris, 2008, p. 29.

subjects so badly, to see the French commit faults not just out of ignorance, foolishness, or lack of wisdom, which is excusable, but commit faults that go against justice and morality, which isn't excusable. . . . My letters have all become lamentations. I love our Africa, I love France, I love our Tuareg. I see all that we could do. But instead of moving forward I see that we are only regressing. Less than that could make you sad. We will end up losing Africa deplorably, disgracefully. And it will be our own fault because we neglected our duty![154]

Although brother Charles was keenly aware of the evil effects of colonialism, he never questioned colonization itself, France's right to occupy another land. Ali Merad, an Algerian Muslim, discussed as much in his book *Christian Hermit in an Islamic World.*

From a strictly Algerian point of view, it may appear justifiable to consider Father de Foucauld's attitude in critical terms. There are good grounds for this: on the one hand, there are the political views of the former officer, who remained to the end a supporter of French expansionism in Africa; on the other hand, there is his actual solidarity with the colonial regime, the true nature of which had doubtless escaped him.

In spite of everything, it seems to us unjust to blame a monk like Charles de Foucauld for not being able to transcend the outlook of his time. . . . The truth demands that Charles de Foucauld be considered in a context that was truly his own; not that of an officer, a colonial administrator or an ideologue, but purely in a spiritual context. In this context, de

---

154. Letter to Henri Laperrine, January 7, 1913.

Foucauld has left his mark as an exemplary figure.
. . . Living among the Tuareg, he shared their lot,
seeing them not as strangers but as neighbours,
friends and brothers. His dedication to the Tuareg
people and to the country of his adoption would
endure until his death.[155]

The Fraternity of the Sacred Heart wasn't situated
in some quiet haven, but on one of humanity's fault lines
at the beginning of the twentieth century, at a time when
Europe was pursuing an aggressive expansion whose
consequences it is still reaping today. The universal little
brother, like his universal elder Brother, had his feet sol-
idly planted in this real world, with all that that implies.
Jacques Maritain, who became a little brother towards
the end of his life, wrote: "You cannot touch human flesh
without soiling your fingers. But soiling your fingers is
not the same thing as soiling your heart."[156]

---

155. Ali Merad, *Christian Hermit in an Islamic World*, New York:
Paulist Press, 1999, p. 72.
156. Jacques Maritain, *Humanisme Intégrale*, Paris: Éditions
Montaigne, 1968, p. 252.

6

A Spirituality of the Visitation

The good we do is commensurate with what we are, not what we do or say.[157]

In the silence of the desert, brother Charles's grave bears the telling inscription, "I want to cry the Gospel with my whole life." They are not exactly his words, but they summarize what he wanted to live: evangelization not through words but through a way of being. He drew his inspiration from the Visitation. Mary had entered Elizabeth's house not with a speech but with just a greeting. What she carried within awoke what Elizabeth bore deep inside. This concept of mission inspired a whole generation under the auspices of the Catholic Action movement, which sought to witness to the gospel in a society that was distancing itself from the institutional Church. Today, in a world where encounter easily becomes confrontation, this approach can help foster a fruitful fellowship between religions. Brother Charles was a precursor of the "dialogue of life."

The Discovery of the mystery of the Visitation

Brother Charles chose the Visitation as the patron feast of the Little Brothers and Sisters of the Sacred Heart of Jesus. He saw it as an icon of the contemplative vocation in mission countries.

---

157. Rule for the Union of Brothers and Sisters of the Sacred Heart, Article XXVIII, No. 3.

When doubts about his calling as a Trappist began to surface, he gained a sudden insight into his *special vocation* as he contemplated the Visitation. On January 2, 1899, he wrote to Fr. Huvelin:

> About five and a half years ago I told you . . . that my dream was to imitate the Blessed Virgin in the mystery of the Visitation. Like her, I would silently bring Jesus and the exercise of the evangelical virtues, but not to the house of St. Elizabeth. I would go among non-Christians so as to sanctify them by the presence of the Blessed Sacrament and the example of Christian virtues.

In the Visitation, two movements that appeared to draw him in opposite directions came together. The first was a call to live in silence, alone with God alone. The image of this was Mary silently contemplating Jesus present in her womb. Charles always considered this to be his vocation and it was in harmony with his temperament. The other movement found its expression in the word *brother* and urged him to go out and find Jesus in the least of his brothers and sisters. It was illustrated by Mary setting off in haste to meet her aged cousin, Elizabeth. Brother Charles sometimes felt torn between what he felt to be his vocation and what seemed to be God's will. Yet it was precisely this tension which would lead him to sanctity.

The Visitation: silent evangelization

When he looked back on his life, Charles realized that Jesus Christ had visited him in his own cousin. She had brought the Lord to him, overcoming the stalemate to which his purely intellectual search for truth had led him. He addressed Jesus, saying, "You came to me, borne by another Mary, bounding over all obstacles as you once bounded over the hills and valleys of Israel, sanctifying me without my doing anything."[158]

The strength of his cousin's testimony rested on her way of being. "A beautiful soul seconded your work, my God, but by her silence, her gentleness, and her goodness. She let herself be seen. She was good, spreading her fragrant perfume, but she did not intervene! You, my Jesus, my Savior did everything both within and outside! You drew me to virtue by the beauty of a soul in whom virtue appeared so exquisite that it ravished my heart forever."[159]

Her life spread its *perfume*. Brother Charles was fond of that metaphor.

> Let us imitate Jesus. . . . Let us be his instruments as Mary was. This mystery illustrates the duties of contemplatives towards non-Christians . . . a life that *is fragrant* with all the evangelical virtues. . . . O my God, I always believed you wanted this of me; make me fulfill it according to your will! Amen.[160]

Perfume attracts. Its effect has nothing to do with logic or effort, but makes you lose your senses like good wine! Brother Charles put a quote from the Song of Songs at the beginning of his 1896 Rule: "Delicate is the fragrance of your perfume. Draw me in your footsteps, let us run!"[161] If the little brothers allowed themselves to be drawn by this perfume, they would run without effort and their lives would spread the same fragrance.

---

158. Meditation on Luke 1:39-56, 1898.
159. Notes from retreat in Nazareth, November 8, 1898.
160. Meditation on Luke 1:39-56, 1898.
161. Song of Songs 1:4; translated from Charles de Foucauld's writings.

Evangelii Gaudium recalls that "It is not by prose-
lytizing that the Church grows but by attraction" (20). In
her 1969 diary, little sister Magdeleine quoted Gandhi's
words to a missionary:

> The best way to preach the Gospel of Christ is to live
> it. I like those who do not preach but practice what
> they believe. Their lives are silent and yet they give
> real witness.

> A rose has no need to preach. It simply spreads its
> fragrance. Its fragrance is its sermon. That is why
> I say to you, let your life itself speak to us, like the
> rose which has no need of words but simply gives
> off its scent. Even the blind man who can't see the
> rose is attracted by its perfume. This is the secret of
> what I would call the "gospel of the rose." But the
> Gospel which Jesus preached has a perfume much
> more exquisite and much more penetrating than the
> gospel of the rose.

Good perfume radiates with the warmth of the body.
It first needs to become one with the body in order for its
fragrance to be diffused. Using imagery from the Visitation, one might say that you need to be pregnant with
Jesus in order to carry him to others. In the Visitation two
pregnant women meet. Each carries a life which doesn't
belong to her, but what each one bears speaks to what is
most hidden in the other.

When he first settled in Beni Abbès, brother Charles
began to adopt the White Fathers' style of mission. He
attempted to create a little Christian community with a
few redeemed slaves and an old lady, Marie, whom he had
baptized *in extremis*. He composed a catechism for their
use: *The Gospel Presented to the Poor of the Sahara*. But
very quickly he realized that before catechizing, you need

to create bonds with people, to make yourself known. Nazareth meant a mission that didn't rely on works but on life. The deciding factor in the proclamation of the gospel was the quality of the messenger.

> The good we do is commensurate with what we are, not what we do or say. It depends on the grace that accompanies our actions, the extent to which Jesus lives in us, to which our actions are His, acting in and through us. . . . The good wrought by a person is directly proportionate to his or her holiness. May this truth always be present to our minds.[162]

Going out to others

The Visitation implies silent evangelization by one's life *and* going out towards others. During the papal conclave in March 2013, Jorge Mario Bergoglio recalled the urgency of *going out* for the Church's mission today.

> When the Church does not come out from itself to evangelize it becomes self-referential and gets sick. . . . In Revelation, Jesus says that he is standing at the threshold and calling. Evidently the text refers to the fact that he stands outside the door and knocks to enter. . . . But at times I think that Jesus may be knocking from the inside, that we may let him out.[163]

Mary sets off immediately, even if prudence might have dictated otherwise. The need to announce is char-

---

162. Rule for the Union of Brothers and Sisters of the Sacred Heart, Art XXVIII, No. 3.

163. "Benedict and Francis: A Lesson in Continuity," The Catholic World Report, May 6, 2013, accessed online.

acteristic of Christianity. As soon as Philip meets Jesus
he needs to find Nathanael. The Samaritan woman leaves
her jar at the well in her haste to go tell those in her village about the one she has just encountered. One gets the
impression that it is only in announcing Christ to others
that you fully receive him. Jesus is *sent* by the Father, and
those who receive him become *sent* themselves. That is
why brother Charles saw Christ, not Mary, as the protag-
onist in the Visitation. On that feast day in 1898 he wrote:

> Oh! my mother . . . the Visitation is one of your
> beloved feast days, though it's Our Lord's feast more
> than yours because He is the one acting in you. The
> Visitation is "the charity of Christ urging you on."

> What Mary undertakes in the Visitation isn't a visit
> to her cousin so that they might console and edify
> each other . . . even less is it a charitable visit to
> help her during her last few months of pregnancy
> and labor. It's so much more than that. She sets off
> to sanctify and evangelize St. John, not by words but
> by silently bringing him Jesus, right in the midst of
> his own house. The same is done by monks and nuns
> vowed to contemplation in mission countries.[164]

One could judge these words to be those of a man
insensitive to the difficulties related to a pregnancy late
in life! But what brother Charles writes squares with the
Gospel narrative. If the main reason for Mary's visit to her
cousin had been to help her it would have been normal that
she remain until the baby's birth. Strangely, Luke records
Mary's departure before narrating the birth of John the
Baptist. Her visit seems to have been simply to greet her
cousin. That's where the text places the emphasis:

164. Meditation, Nazareth, July 2, 1898.

She entered the house of Zechariah and *greeted* Elizabeth. And when Elizabeth heard the *greeting* of Mary, the babe leaped in her womb; and Elizabeth was filled with the Holy Spirit. . . . "For behold, when the voice of your *greeting* came to my ears, the babe in my womb leaped for joy."[165]

Mary herself had been visited by an angel who had greeted her with the words, "Hail, full of grace, the Lord is with you!" She had "considered in her mind what sort of *greeting* this might be" and soon after set off for her cousin's, urged by a Word that had taken flesh in her.[166] Brother Charles wanted to be taken up in that same movement.

O my mother, grant that we be faithful to this divine mission! . . . Help us perpetually, grant us your all powerful help and the grace of ceaselessly asking it of you, O Mother of Perpetual Help, so that, in the midst of these poor infidels, we might do what you did in Zechariah's house.[167]

Going in haste

Brother Charles noted that Mary set off to Elizabeth's as quickly as she could. "When you are full of Jesus, you are full of charity. You go out to those you want to save like Jesus went to them by becoming incarnate. What is good is done with haste because charity urges us and will admit no delay."[168] Appealing for help to start his confraternity, he wrote:

---

165. Luke 1:40-44, emphasis added.
166. Luke 1:28,29, emphasis added.
167. Meditation, Nazareth, July 2, 1898.
168. Meditation on Luke 1:39, June 1916.

The Sahara, which is 8 or 10 times bigger than France, with a bigger population than had been thought, has only 13 priests. The Moroccan highlands are as big as France, with a population of 8 to 10 million, and yet there is not a single Tabernacle or altar.

Our Lord is in a hurry. . . . The days given to love him, imitate him, save souls with him, pass, and we do not love him, do not imitate him, do not save.[169]

On his clock he had inscribed the words, "It is time to love God." They expressed his awareness that time was given to us so that we might love, and that love always acts with haste. Jesus' heart burned with love for all people. That same fire had been kindled in the heart of his little brother, and when there's fire you need to act quickly!

An exposed life

Brother Charles saw himself going to the people of the Sahara like Mary in the Visitation. She carried Jesus in her womb and Charles carried him in the Blessed Sacrament. The Eucharist was the very reason for his presence among these faraway populations. Shortly after settling there he wrote to his cousin, "Is my presence here of any use? If it isn't, there is the Blessed Sacrament which certainly generates a lot of good."[170]

Before his departure for Tamanrasset, Msgr. Guérin had questioned Charles. Liturgical norms required the presence of a second Christian to celebrate the Eucharist. So long as he was on tour with a French convoy, he could find someone willing to serve his

---

169. Letter to Suzanne Perret, December 15, 1904.
170. Letter to Marie de Bondy, November 18, 1907.

Mass. But if he settled there, he would be alone, so what would he do? Brother Charles sent his reply on the feast of the Visitation.

> The question which you put: Is it better to live in the Hoggar without being able to celebrate Holy Mass, or to celebrate it and not go there? I have often asked myself this question. Being the only priest able to go to the Hoggar, while many can celebrate the Holy Sacrifice, I believe it is, after all, better to go to the Hoggar, leaving it to God to give me the means of celebrating, if He wishes. . . . Formerly I was inclined always to sacrifice everything to the celebration of Holy Mass. But this reasoning must be faulty somewhere, since, from the time of the Apostles, in certain circumstances, the greatest saints have sacrificed the possibility of celebrating to works of spiritual charity, such as travelling, etc. If experience were to show that in being in Tamanrasset, I would have long stretches without Mass, then I would need to shorten my stays, but not attempt to go around with military detachments, *which is not at all the same thing as residing alone.* Living alone in a place is a good thing. You achieve something even if you don't do much, because you start to belong to the country. You're approachable and unimposing there: it gives you such *littleness*.[171]

It was a remarkable step forward in his thinking, which in no way diminished his attachment to the Blessed Sacrament. Quite to the contrary! The months spent in Tamanrasset without being able to celebrate Mass were a time of great distress. During his first Christmas he wrote to his cousin:

---

171. Bazin, p. 260.

Christmas. This night no Mass for the first time in twenty-one years. May the Beloved's will be done. . . . In His mercy He still leaves me the Blessed Sacrament. . . . Up to the last minute I had hoped that somebody would come, but no one did, neither a Christian traveller, nor a soldier; nor did permission come to celebrate alone. It's been three months, over three months since I received a letter.[172]

The dispensation to celebrate Mass, which he practically despaired of ever receiving, was granted him six months later, by the pope himself, during an audience with the White Fathers' procurator. In giving him the news, however, Msgr. Guérin had to inform him that Church norms did not permit him to reserve the Blessed Sacrament. With brother Charles being so isolated, it was a question of what would happen to it in the event of his death. Thus, for six and a half years, even if he had the right to celebrate Mass, his tabernacle remained empty.[173]

This eucharistic fast was an enormous trial for a man who lived in such isolated conditions and whose love for the Eucharist could be summed up in the word *Presence*. But as brother Antoine Chatelard has written, it would make him undergo the transition from "exposition of the Blessed Sacrament" to an "exposed" life. It was among Muslims that brother Charles had had a taste of the greatness of God, and had witnessed the human response that is worship. It left its stamp on his spiritual itinerary. But the Christian God seeks more than worship: he seeks friendship. That is why brother Charles wrote to his apostolic prefect, "Living alone in a place is a good thing. You

---

172. Letter to Marie de Bondy, Christmas 1907.
173. In 1914 the new apostolic prefect would understand that permission to celebrate Mass alone included permission to reserve the Blessed Sacrament.

achieve something even if you don't do much, because you start to belong to the country." Familiarity makes friendship possible. His life would be the only Eucharist his *Muslim parishioners* would ever know.

Belonging to the country

Crying the gospel with his life demanded that brother Charles make himself close to his neighbors, down to the most concrete details of their lives. A French journalist who visited him in Tamanrasset joked about Charles's diet in a letter to his fiancée:

> Father eats cracked wheat (not ground, as that would make a pasty glue) boiled up as gruel with a bit of butter, or kesra (unleavened Arab bread—heavy as a brick!) dipped in date purée. He continually alternates between these two dishes (!) and though the first is edible, you'd rather die of hunger than eat the second! He has a cast-iron stomach![174]

When he was young, his fasting had made a deep impression on the people around him; but in a context where his neighbors subsisted on a meager diet all year round, it meant something completely different. He wrote to a Trappist who had made inquiries about his life, regarding his decision to *belong to the country*.

> Food here is completely different than in Europe. Introducing European food here would be an expensive luxury. Don't even think about it, but live like other people, from what the country produces:

---

174. Félix Dubois, "Visit to Charles de Foucauld," *Bulletin des Amitiés Charles de Foucauld*, April 1996, no. 122, p. 6.

wheat, dates, dairy products; same thing for clothing and lodging. You will only find the poorest and most basic, nothing that resembles the neat, fashionable clothing and houses of France.[175]

Next to his hermitage in Tamanrasset, he built a *zriba* which he dubbed his refectory!

The art of conversation

As he grew in understanding of his vocation, brother Charles began to refer to himself as a *missionary monk*, living an *apostolate of friendship*. Conversation was its privileged instrument. "I never hesitate to prolong conversations and let them last very long when I see that they are useful. Sometimes I spend entire days explaining and showing books of holy pictures or reading passages of the holy Gospel in Tuareg."[176] His goal in these conversations was to lead people to their better selves by addressing their conscience and appealing to those truths that flowed from their natural sense of religion. Love helped him discover how to go about speaking to each person.

> Let us not forget that souls are different and that, following God's example, you have to draw some people one way, others another, guide some in one manner, others in another, each according to what God has put inside of them. It would be madness to have only one method and want everyone to conform. You need to study people and lead them to God, each according to the way in which God calls them.[177]

---

175. Letter to Fr. Antonin, May 13, 1911.
176. Letter to Msgr. Guérin, March 6, 1908.
177. Meditation on Psalm 51, Nazareth, 1897.

He no longer approached people as a caregiver, as he did in Beni Abbès, but as a friend. His apostolate of friendship was in imitation of the One who made himself close to each human being, revealing the pleasure God takes in entering into conversation with each one.

Brother Charles left traces of his conversations with Moussa. He would prepare them carefully because, since Moussa was a nomad, Charles never knew when he would drop by. He kept a list of "Things to say to Moussa" of which the following are a few examples:

- Reduce expenses. Be humble. God alone is great. He who thinks himself great, or who seeks to be great, does not know God.

- *Never lie to anybody.* All untruth is hateful to God, for God is truth.

- Never praise a person to his face. When one loves and esteems someone, it is demonstrated by one's actions and one's trust; there is no use in talking about it. To flatter someone is contemptible.[178]

He also practiced his apostolate by conversation with Christians. Dr. Hérisson recalls:

Before sunset, Father took an hour's recreation. He used to walk to and fro before his hermitage. Then he talked amiably of everything. We walked side by side. He put his hand on my shoulder, laughed, spoke about the Tuareg and his memories. At first he used to ask me every time how I had spent the day. He got me to make a sort of examination of conscience,

---

178. Bazin, p. 244.

and blamed me if I had not attended to some Tuareg, learned Arabic or Tamahaq.[179]

What did his Muslim friends think?

One might wonder what the inhabitants of the Sahara understood of the visit that God was paying them in the Christian marabout. Brother Charles often asked himself that question. After his prefect's visit to Beni Abbès he noted:

> In order to bring the Muslims to God, do you need to seek their esteem by excelling in certain things that they value? For example, by being bold, a good horseman, a lavish giver, etc. Or should you practice the Gospel in its abjection and its poverty, trudging along on foot without luggage, doing manual work like JESUS in Nazareth, living poorly like a lowly labourer? . . . The Muslims don't make a mistake in this matter. When they see a priest who's a good horse rider, good marksman, etc., they say: "He's an excellent rider, no one can shoot as well as him." But they don't say he's a saint. . . . Should a missionary lead the life of St. Anthony in the desert, they will all say, "He's a saint." Natural reason will often make them friends of the former; but when it comes to matters regarding their souls, they will only trust the latter.[180]

During his trip to France with Oûksem in 1913, his Tuareg friends wrote to him. There are about twenty of

---

179. Ibid., p. 288.
180. Notes after Msgr. Guérin's visit, Béni Abbès, June 19, 1903.

these letters and they allow us to sense the relationship from their point of view.

> It's me Chikat who says: I send a lot of greetings to my companion the marabout.
> It's me Choumekki who says: I address a lot of greetings to the marabout and his sister.
> Everyone is well. We have no news (of you).
> It's me Oûksem who says, I send a lot of greetings to the marabout.
> It's me Abahag who says, I send a lot of greetings to the marabout.
> It's me Litni the kalipha who says, I send a lot of greetings to the marabout.
> It's me Aflan who says, I send a lot of greetings to my father the marabout.
> It's me Abdelqadir who says, I send a lot of greetings to the marabout.
> It's me Adhan who says, I send a lot of greetings to the marabout.
> It's me Adhan who says, I send a lot of greetings to Oûksem.
> It's me Oûksem who says, I send a lot of greetings to my namesake.
> It's me Adhan who says: Mokhammed ag Chikat had a son. He still doesn't have a name.[181]

This shower of greetings recalls the Visitation. In a society that depends on oral tradition, words are very important in interpersonal relationships. They are not meant to convey information so much as to express benevolence, acknowledging how good it is that the other person exists.

---

181. *Lettres au Marabout*, p. 132.

Evangelized by the Muslims

Mary was changed by the Visitation. The recognition by Elizabeth of what she carried within changed the young girl from Nazareth into the woman who proclaims the Magnificat. Brother Charles was also changed through his life with his Muslim parishioners. True encounters always sharpen our own sense of identity.

During the famine in 1908, brother Charles fell ill with scurvy. It was not the first time, but now he was almost at death's door. He knew that milk could help him. But what could he do? "The goats are as dry as the earth is, and the people as dry as the goats."[182] The Tuareg women who came to see him went in search of all the goats in a radius of three miles so as to bring him what was most precious in this time of famine: a bit of milk. General Laperrine spoke of it in a letter to Msgr. Guérin:

> Reverend Father, a few lines dashed off in a hurry, to give you news of de Foucauld. He's putting off his journey till October. He has been more ill than he admits; he had fainting fits, and the Tuareg who took great care of him are very anxious. He is better. I lambasted him, for I am strongly of the opinion that his exaggerated penances have a great deal to do with his weakness, and the overwork on his dictionary did the rest.[183]

Thanks to that moment of weakness, the bond with the Tuareg metamorphosed into a reciprocal relationship. Now a true friendship could blossom. He later wrote to Henri de Castries: "I spent all of 1912 here, in this hamlet of Tamanrasset. The Tuareg are very con-

---

182. Letter to Marie de Bondy, July 17, 1907.
183. Bazin, p. 266.

soling company. I cannot express how good they are for me, how many upright souls I find among them; one or two of them are real friends, something that is everywhere so rare and so precious."[184]

Brother Charles had a notebook where he kept a record of all the European visitors he received in Tamanrasset, but as of 1913 he started noting Tuareg visitors as well. In 1914, one of those he classed among his "real friends" came down with malaria. Brother Charles had known Abahag since he first arrived in Tamanrasset in 1905, but it had taken a while for the relationship to develop. He wrote to his cousin on March 18, 1906: "During the winter the Tuareg do not go out much. They are sensitive to cold and they have no warm clothing. Besides, they're not in much of a hurry to visit me. The ice needs to be broken." Relations warmed up in 1907, when Abahag served as a guide for the tour around Adrar in which brother Charles participated. His name appeared in Charles's notebook for the first time in 1908. In a letter to Brigadier Garnier in 1913, Abahag was named among the four friends he could really count on in Tamanrasset. "How did they become my friends? In the same way that we form bonds among ourselves. I don't give them any presents; but they understood that they had a friend in me, that I was true, that they could trust me, and they have reciprocated the same attitude towards me."[185]

In general, brother Charles jotted things in his notebook briefly and concisely, but on learning of Abahag's illness, he became more detailed. "October 23, 1914—Tonight I found out that Abahag has been unconscious since last evening. He suddenly developed a very high, pernicious fever. He had had a bit of fever earlier but it didn't seem very serious." The next day he noted, "October 24,

---

184. Letter to Henri de Castries, January 8, 1913.
185. Letter to Brig. Garnier, February 23, 1913.

1914. Abahag died today around 4 in the afternoon. He was buried at 6 pm. Took part in the burial."

That very evening, he took the sealed envelope containing his own last will and testament and wrote on the back: "I wish to be buried where I die, a simple burial, no coffin, very simple grave, no monument, just a wooden cross. October 24, 1914." Abahag's burial seems to have helped him define how he wanted to live and die. And indeed, the morning after Charles's death the village people gave him a "very simple" burial.

The joy of the Visitation

The story of the Visitation is suffused with joy. Those who knew brother Charles often mentioned his joy. When Dr. Hérisson asked him for advice on how to approach the Tuareg, Charles replied:

> Be human, charitable, *and always joyful*. You must always laugh, even in saying the simplest things. I, as you see, am always laughing, showing my horrible teeth. Laughter puts the person you are talking to in a good mood; it draws people closer together, allows them to understand each other better; it sometimes brightens up a gloomy character, it is a charity.[186]

Where did that joy come from? Certainly, it flowed from his life in God, but surely it also came to him from the "very consoling company" he kept with his Tuareg friends. Brother Charles reminds us that the Church rediscovers her joy and youth when she crosses the institutional threshold and goes out to meet the men and women of our world.

---

186. Bazin, p. 285.

7

An Enduring Perseverance

You ask me if I am willing to go elsewhere than Béni Abbés to spread the holy Gospel: for that I am ready to go to the ends of the earth and to live until the last judgement.[187]

During the meal following the Mass that concluded the recent Year for Consecrated Life in the diocese of Westminster, a little sister pointed out the new auxiliary bishop to me, saying, "He really loves brother Charles; he included him in the litany of saints during his consecration." Later on, I met him on the way out, and so I introduced myself, and asked what brother Charles meant to him. He paused, and then speaking straight from the heart, he said, "It's his enduring perseverance. He makes such huge efforts; the results are practically nil but he just keeps going." I was touched by his words because it gave me an insight to his own experience of ministry, which, in fact, is that of many people in the Church today. Efforts are huge but the results are slender indeed. Where is the miraculous catch of fish promised to those in Peter's boat?

In recommending brother Charles for a mission in the Sahara, Fr. Huvelin had written of him, "A tough instrument for a hard job."[188] His efforts would be enormous in every domain: the rules he wrote in the hope that companions would come, his work on the dictionary to preserve Tuareg culture and enable it to resist Arabisation, his appeals that France commit itself to improving the spiritual and material lot of

187. Letter to Msgr. Guérin, February 27, 1903.
188. Fr. Huvelin to Msgr. Livinhac, September 5, 1901.

its colonies, and his quest to win the trust of the indigenous population. All of these appeared to yield very little fruit. He was fond of quoting St. John of the Cross: "We should not match the work we do to our weakness, but match our efforts to the work that must be done."[189] He had already demonstrated that he was a *tough instrument* during his exploration of Morocco. In his report to the annual general meeting of the Paris Geographical Society, which awarded Charles its gold medal on April 24, 1885, Henri Duveyrier stated, "The Viscount de Foucauld returned to Algeria after crossing Morocco from north to south and from southwest to northeast. To do that, he gave up much more than a few comforts, completely taking on several vows' worth of poverty and misery."[190] He was a true de Foucauld, worthy of the family motto, "Never retreat." Faith would heighten this natural disposition, putting it at the service of the gospel.

An absence of companions

Brother Charles had great ambitions on arriving at Beni Abbès. The Fraternity of the Sacred Heart, which he planned down to the minutest details, was not a small-scale affair. He wrote to Dom Martin, "I have paid for the land. It includes about 22 acres, plenty of water, 180 palm trees, and quite a few other fruit trees. These suffice to occupy and feed twenty to thirty monks, who could garden and tend the fruit trees. It would be enough to meet their needs since the number of palm trees, which are a good source of revenue, could be greatly increased."[191]

---

189. Letter to Fr. Caron, June 9, 1908.
190. Pierre Sourisseau, *Bulletin des Amitiés Charles de Foucauld*, October 1983, no. 72, p. 12.
191. Letter to Dom Martin, April 24, 1902.

While in Nazareth, he had written the rule for his future community of little brothers. It had kept him busy for months because he had had to write out forty articles for both Rule and Constitutions in triplicate, with parts in Latin. He had resolved to establish his first Fraternity "not where, humanly speaking, there are the best chances of getting novices . . . but where it is the most perfect in and of itself."[192] But *the most perfect in and of itself* consisted in the most isolated and difficult conditions possible! He needed, therefore, to rely on the White Fathers and Trappists to find him candidates.

His letters contained frequent appeals, but despite an abundance of vocations in both congregations, those in charge hesitated to send him candidates. The prior of the Trappist monastery in Staouéli wrote to Commander Lacroix, "My only regret is that I have no one I can send to assist him. The superiors of our Order have the greatest affection for him but his life is so austere that they judge him more admirable than imitable. They fear discouragement in any potential candidates they send him."[193] His insistent requests that the Trappists send him brother Augustine, a former *zouave*[194] he had known at Our Lady of the Snows, were unsuccessful. Dom Martin replied, "We cannot send you br. Augustine. We cannot, in conscience, take him out of a religious life approved by the Church and cast him into an undertaking which is certainly pious and admirable, but which, according to some prudent people, is unlikely to meet with success."[195] The only candidate who ever tried his vocation was brother Michel (Goyat), a twenty-three-year-old Breton who had joined the White

---

192. Notes from retreat before priestly ordination, June 1901.

193. Fr. Henri to Commander Lacroix, January 5, 1902.

194. Member of a French infantry unit originally composed of Algerians.

195. Dom Martin to Charles de Foucauld, September 3, 1902.

Fathers but seemed more cut out for a contemplative life. He wrote an account of the three months spent in brother Charles's company. One can read between the lines that it had never occurred to his "venerable superior" that a candidate might need a progressive initiation. Brother Charles went to fetch him in Algiers, and almost immediately set off for Tamanrasset. Michel narrates:

> During the whole crossing of the desert, which took place in winter, the day temperature was from 15° to 20° [Celsius], that of night from four or five degrees below freezing-point. In the morning we sometimes found frozen water in the cruet, and the ground covered with a thin coat of ice. From time to time a violent wind blew and made thick clouds of dust, driving sand into our eyes and small pebbles into our faces. . . . More often we slept under the canopy of heaven without any fire, in a hole large enough to lodge a man's body, which we ourselves hollowed out with our hands in the sand, and which served us as a bed. Benumbed with cold, rolled up in our camp blankets, we tossed and turned again and again on our mats all night, to warm ourselves and induce sleep, but without succeeding. Towards noon we used to halt for a good hour, which enabled us to light a fire for cooking our dinner. A little before sunset at the place where we were to camp, we had supper. . . . I felt seriously ill a little more than two months after our departure from Beni Abbès, and I felt incapable of continuing so toilsome a journey on foot in the sands. I was obliged to stop at In-Salah, and, to my great regret, renounce the Tuareg mission.[196]

---

196. Bazin, p. 252.

Brother Michel finished his life as a Carthusian monk, proof that he was no weakling. But Fr. Henri had not been wrong: brother Charles was more admirable than imitable. Even if, later on, his appeals were for "excellent priests who are of mature age," no one came. The absence of companions tormented him; he blamed himself and his slow conversion to Jesus' way of thinking. He wrote to Dom Martin, "I lack two things: brothers and myself. Myself, meaning my conversion, because my conversion would attract brothers. You are waiting for my conversion before you send me brother Augustine. You don't trust me, and you are right not to, because I am a miserable sinner, guilty of hundreds of acts of cowardice, infidelity, and half-heartedness. Pray for my conversion."[197]

A community down to zero

Failure would not be limited to his hopes for a candidate.

His indignation at the persistence of slavery in Beni Abbès led him to redeem a few young slaves. He was inspired by New Testament passages witnessing to the presence of many slaves among the early Christians. Hoping that they would form the beginnings of a community in Beni Abbès, he wrote to his cousin, "Pray for my four children in Beni Abbès: Abd-Jesu who is still with me and is more and more of a dear, Paul, Pierre, and Marie—feeble beginnings of Christianity in these parts."[198]

But hardly two months later he had to admit to his cousin:

---

197. Letter to Dom Martin, May 15, 1902.
198. Letter to Marie de Bondy, January 21, 1903.

Our little beginnings of Christianity here at Beni Abbès seem to be going back down to zero. May the will of Jesus be done. Paul left me in a rather painful way, and Pierre, whose parents live ten days' walk or so from here, wants to go back to them. Marie is going to have her cataracts operated on and if it works she won't have any more reason to stay and can go back to living on her own. There'll be only Abd-Jesu left, more and more of a dear, and I'm eager to see him in better hands than mine, with the Sisters of St. Vincent de Paul.[199]

Even if his own community baptized orphans and raised them as Christians, Msgr. Guérin had some reservations about this form of evangelization. He wrote to brother Charles on October 31, 1904: "You mustn't forget these children's background and the society to which they must necessarily return. In wanting to go too quickly with their religious or even moral instruction we run a serious risk of spoiling everything, not just for the children themselves but for the future development of the mission." Henceforth brother Charles would address himself to adults.

The exhausting mission among the Tuareg

The mission among the Tuareg entailed huge difficulties. The journey from Algiers to Tamanrasset took a month and a half in the harsh conditions imposed by the Sahara. In his youth, brother Charles had already crossed the desert and he knew what it involved, especially in the company of soldiers. Normal difficulties were compounded by his desire to imitate the first apos-

---

199. Letter to Marie de Bondy, March 2, 1903.

tles who journeyed as poor people. Captain Dinaux, who commanded one of the convoys, recalls:

> After two hours of trekking in the early morning, everybody had mounted their camel except Father, who was praying his rosary or reciting litanies as he trekked along on foot until near exhaustion. It was obvious that he was pushing himself to go faster in all kinds of difficult terrain; from 5 am the sun would start beating down on us mercilessly, the temperature in the shade was between 40° and 50° [Celsius]. Each of us was drinking from 8 to 10 liters a day, but what water! It was often tainted with magnesium, or drawn from pools where herds had waded. Father kept following with his quick steps until the wind began to blow a storm or one of us would say to him, "Father, if you don't mount, I will dismount and walk beside you." So then he would put an end to his ordeal, give us a lovely smile, and chat about all kinds of subjects until we reached the campsite.[200]

During his first year on tour he covered nearly four thousand miles, and it has been estimated that in all, he spent four years of his life trekking in the Sahara. Laperrine remembers:

> It's not with distances that you are going to frighten de Foucauld, who can devour an incredible number of kilometers. . . . He usually travels at a rate of 50 km [about thirty miles] a day, doing 25-30 by foot and the rest on a camel. . . . If we were setting off early morning for a full day of walking he would say his

---

200. General Dinaux, "L'Installation du Père de Foucauld au Hoggar," *Cahiers Charles de Foucauld*, Lyon: Éditions Arthaud, 1947, no. 4, p. 40.

Mass at 2 am. If, to the contrary, we were planning to walk the whole night so that man and beast could rest during the heat of the day, he would celebrate on arrival, usually around midday. He used to nibble on a few dates around 11 pm as he walked and that would keep him going until after his Mass.[201]

The re-Islamization of the Hoggar

Ironically, it was the French occupation of the Sahara which, by putting an end to the anarchy that reigned in the Hoggar, allowed the Tuareg to return to the Muslim religion of their fathers. Moussa ag Amastane, named *amenokal* by France in 1904, had come under the sway of Cheikh Beï, a Kunta[202] marabout. When he was young he had taken advantage of the spiritual direction Cheikh Beï offered. In his short biography of Moussa, brother Charles wrote, "a great change came about in his life. He had been converted. Under Beï's advice . . . he said good-bye to a life of pillaging and of *courtly soirées*, consecrating his efforts to working for peace."[203] Out of fidelity to his master, Moussa accepted the presence of the French on condition that it allow him to redirect his people toward God.

This re-Islamization took place during brother Charles's own lifetime. Returning to Tamanrasset after a ten-month absence, he wrote to Msgr. Livinhac, superior general of the White Fathers: "I found the Hoggar quite changed. The biggest difference is its organization into

---

201. Henri Laperrine, "The Stages in the Conversion of a Houzard," *Revue de Cavalerie*, October 1913.
202. Tribes living in northern Mali, Mauritania, and Niger.
203. *Poésies Touarègues*, published by André Basset, Leroux: Paris, 1925, Vol. 1, p. 366. Charles wrote an introduction to Moussa's poems.

a Muslim state and its Islamization under the direction of the amenokol, Moussa ag Amastane." The latter wanted to make Tamanrasset the capital of his little Muslim state. "He has named a caïd, wants to build a mosque, and establish a *zaouia* where people can learn reading, the Qur'an, and Muslim law."[204] Unfortunately, the caïd squandered the money given him and nothing was built. Brother Charles wrote to his friend, Commander Lacroix, "Beï isn't around to give him sound advice when he needs it."[205] French occupation not only allowed the re-Islamization of the Hoggar but also its Arabization, two scenarios that brother Charles feared. Rather than discouraging him, failure turned him to God.

> Will it be given to the generations that come after us to see the multitudes of North Africa say together, "Our Father who art in heaven" . . . I do not know. It is the secret of God. But it is our duty to work towards it with all our strength.[206]

And he wanted a lot of other people to commit themselves to working with that same ardor.

The Union of the Brothers and Sisters of the Sacred Heart: an uphill battle

Convinced that the presence of sisters among the Tuareg would be very beneficial, brother Charles sought the help of Mother Augustine, superior of the White Sisters in Ghardaïa. "Since the Beloved granted both of us a vocation working in His field of the Sahara, I took advantage

---

204. Letter to Msgr. Livinhac, July 24, 1907.
205. Letter to Commander Lacroix, November 26, 1907.
206. Letter to Henri de Castries, December 10, 1911.

of my weeks in the oases of Gourara and Touat to inquire from those likely to know, whether the White Sisters could open a house among the Tuareg."[207] Unfortunately, tension between the Church and the Republic put those plans on standby.

He later dreamt of the presence of religious or lay people among the local population, so the people could see what Christianity looked like in daily life. It would be a remedy for the evils of colonization. "What the local people see of us Christians who profess a religion of love, what they see of French atheists crying *Fraternity* from the rooftops, is either negligence, ambition, or greed— and from almost all of them indifference, antipathy, and harshness."[208] He wrote to Msgr. Guérin, "That's why I would see apostolic workers coming 'incognito,' in lay clothing, working as merchants or cultivators, secretly bringing JESUS to far away places. . . . It's no different from the life of the early Christians, Paul who made tents, Peter bringing a sister with him."[209]

He corresponded with a certain Mr. Lutoslawski in the hope of attracting Polish immigrants to come to the Sahara rather than going to America. He really knew how to dream the impossible dream! Later his hopes of attracting lay Christians to the Sahara broadened into a plan for a confraternity where the majority of members would remain in their own country but commit themselves through prayer and the practice of the "Nazareth virtues" to the evangelization of indigenous people in the colonies. He sought to make people aware of the extreme destitution he witnessed so that they would take action. One senses both his humility and the ardor of his desires in his letters to Msgr. Guérin:

---

207. Letter to Mother Augustine, February 7, 1905.
208. Letter to Fr. Huvelin, January 1, 1908.
209. Letter to Msgr. Guérin, March 21, 1905.

Forgive me, beloved Father, for meddling in what isn't my business. I am an old sinner, a sinful and miserable, poor little priest, who was only recently ordained. I have never succeeded at anything, never been able to have even one companion, never had anything but desires that came to nothing. My Constitutions and Rules have never been more than useless pieces of paper . . . and yet I dare to expose my thoughts to you and keep making plans. . . . My excuse is the souls around me going to perdition, who will remain in this state perpetually if we don't seek out and take means for persuasive action. The reason for going about this with haste . . . is the simple price of souls, worth the blood Jesus poured out for them.[210]

Brother Charles returned to France in 1909 in the hopes of getting his Union of the Brothers and Sisters of the Sacred Heart started. He consulted his bishop Msgr. Bonnet and Fr. Huvelin. Both endorsed his project but recommended that he entrust its execution to a priest in France, leaving him free to return to the Sahara. They saw him more in an inspirational role than as a founder. He agreed: "I consider myself less capable of tackling this enterprise than almost any other priest, having learned only how to pray in solitude, keep silence, live with books, and at most, chat intimately one-on-one with poor people."[211] That opinion of himself was ratified by Joseph Hours, one of the first members of the Union. He was disappointed with his first meeting with brother Charles in Lyon.

Basically, M. de Foucauld seems to have lost the habit of speech, of conversation, and of discussion. He has become a totally silent contemplative.

---

210. Letter to Msgr. Guérin, June 1, 1908.
211. Letter to Fr. Voillard, June 11, 1916.

He gives the impression of being a true saint, but a modest saint who remains hidden, very humble—not at all an energetic apostle like St. Paul: active, mystic, and claiming his rights as a Roman citizen.

He is a mine of information, supplying fascinating, little known facts about Tuareg, the future of the region, the crossing of the Sahara, and the definitive establishment of French authority in the area. But you have to tear this information out of his mouth bit by bit.[212]

The establishment of the Union would meet with all kinds of obstacles, beginning with that of finding a priest capable and willing to commit himself to it. Msgr. Guérin finally volunteered, but he died in 1910. Having returned to Tamanrasset, brother Charles drew up thirty-nine pages of statutes, inspired by his own rule. At the head of the document he placed a letter from his bishop, Msgr. Bonnet, under the title *Approbation*. The White Fathers' printing press had already produced five hundred copies before a letter arrived from Msgr. Bonnet stating that his Approbation was valid only within his own diocese. Outside of it, permission needed to come from Rome. Rome, for its part, never replied to his request for an Approbation because the Union only existed on paper!

Given all these difficulties, Msgr. Bonnet finally asked brother Charles to try to gather fifty names so as to give his confraternity the beginnings of an existence. The list of the first members practically follows the course of his journey in France in 1913, with friends and family signing up. The first to join was his cousin Louis' parish priest. Charles inscribed himself ninth, to replace his

---

212. Notes written by Joseph Hours after their meeting, July 31, 1913.

cousin Edouard de Morlaincourt, who had given permission to use his name "in case you're short." He just managed to get the fifty names because the bishop's secretary also agreed to be included. But the following year, war put all his plans on hold.

Converting to the methods of Jesus

Despite his temperament—*a tough instrument for a hard job*—the transition from his dream to reality was at times bitter. He often blamed his failure on his own inadequacy. During his pacification tours among the Tuareg he wrote to Msgr. Guérin: "Nothing new here. I don't see a lot of people although there is a bit more familiarity. The people don't like me, but they have become used to seeing me. It takes time. Above all, I would need to be other than I am and finally begin to convert."[213] Christmas 1907 would see him at an all-time low. He had settled in Tamanrasset but didn't have the right to celebrate Mass, Paul having run away once again. Motylinski had died, leaving him alone before a gigantic linguistic enterprise. Michel had not lasted. Moussa was planning to build a mosque in Tamanrasset. Charles's health was failing. In his extreme solitude he wrote to Fr. Huvelin: "You know my wretchedness, you know how much I need your prayers. Over 21 years since you brought me back to Jesus. . . . What a harvest I should have reaped both for myself and for others! But instead of that, only destitution and wretchedness for myself and not the least good for others. . . . A tree is known by its fruit, and that shows me for what I am."[214] The conversion he pined for would not come through greater effort, but would be the fruit of *abandonment*. He

---

213. Letter to Msgr. Guérin, July 15, 1906.
214. Letter to Fr. Huvelin, November 22, 1907.

gradually came to identify his apparently sterile efforts with *Jesus' own efforts*, which conferred on them a new kind of fruitfulness.

> The means Jesus used at His birth in the Manger, at Nazareth, and on the Cross, are these: poverty, utter lowliness, humiliation, rejection, persecution, suffering, the cross. These are our arms, the ones used by our divine Bridegroom, who asks us to let Him continue His life in us. Let us follow Him as our only model and we are sure to do much good, for in that case it will not be we who live but He who lives in us. Our acts will no longer be our own, human and frail, but His divinely efficacious acts.[215]

Abandonment is not a passive acceptance of failure. Rather, it is an attitude that follows an effort as great as one's desire. Brother Charles wrote, "Difficulty is never there in order to stop us. To the contrary, the greater the difficulty, the more urgent it is that you work with all your strength. God always helps those who serve Him. God is always present to us, but so often, it's we who are not present to God!"[216] *He did all he could and then he commended himself to God for the final result.*

It was in the spirit of abandonment that he would come to peacefully accept the lack of companions, which earlier had been such a source of torment. He wrote to Msgr. Guérin:

> If I could do otherwise than surrender wholeheartedly to His divine Will—which is impossible—for my own part, I would prefer total lack of success, perpetual solitude, and failure in all things. "I have

---

215. Letter to Msgr. Guérin, January 15, 1908.
216. Letter to Joseph Hours, May 3, 1912.

chosen abjection." There is a union to abjection and the cross which has always seemed to me desirable beyond all else. I do all I can to have companions (to my mind, the way to get them is to sanctify myself in silence, in the deepest obscurity, like JESUS in Nazareth). If I had some I would rejoice (amidst a lot of worries and crosses!) but not having any, I rejoice perfectly.[217]

He began to view *lack of success* as a means of uniting himself to Jesus and drawing from the fruitfulness of the cross. "If the efforts we make for the salvation of souls meet with no success, the results are that much more blessed for the one who made the efforts, because lack of success increases their resemblance to JESUS. He was hardly listened to, hardly followed, so despised, so scorned, so mocked during His life."[218] One might wonder whether this fundamental aspect of the Christian message hasn't disappeared from the radar for many Christians. The cross has often been reduced to its dolorous aspect, eclipsing its mystical dimension. For brother Charles, "The more firmly we embrace the cross, the more closely we are bound to Jesus."[219]

The prayer of abandonment

Charles de Foucauld is best known for his Prayer of Abandonment, even if he is not its direct author. The prayer is a reformulation of a meditation he wrote at the time of his vocational crisis as a Trappist. Should he make his solemn vows or yield to the persistent voice that called him

217. Letter to Msgr. Guérin, September 30, 1902.
218. Letter to Msgr. Guérin, June 1, 1908.
219. Letter to Louis Massignon, April 5, 1909.

elsewhere? He was pursuing his daily meditation of the Gospel and had arrived at Luke 23:46: "Father, into your hands I commend my spirit." One can guess what he was going through from what he wrote:

> It's the final prayer of our Master, our Beloved. . . . May it also be ours. . . . May it not just be that of our final moment but of every moment: My Father, I surrender myself into your hands; my Father, I entrust myself to you; my Father, I abandon myself to you; my Father, do with me what you will; whatever you may do with me, I thank you; thank you for all; I am ready for all, I accept all; I thank you for all; let only your will be done in me, my God, let only your will be done in all your creatures, in all your children, in all those that your heart loves, I wish no more than this my God; I commend my soul into your hands; I offer it to you my God with all the love of my heart because I love you and it is a need of love to give myself, to surrender myself into your hands without measure; I entrust myself into your hands with infinite confidence, for you are my Father.

When little sister Magdeleine received her first group of novices in 1940, she searched brother Charles's writings for a prayer they might recite every morning that would inspire them with his spirit. Considering the enormous quantity of his meditations, one cannot but appreciate the penetrating intuition with which she seized on this particular meditation, as if she saw in *abandonment* the essence of his spirituality. She and the novices improved the style, removing repetitions to make it suitable for oral recitation. They arrived at the formula which is now so widely known:

Father,
I abandon myself into your hands;
do with me what you will.
Whatever you may do, I thank you:
I am ready for all, I accept all.
Let only your will be done in me,
and in all your creatures.
I wish no more than this, O Lord.
Into your hands I commend my soul;
I offer it to you
with all the love of my heart,
for I love you, Lord,
and so need to give myself,
to surrender myself into your hands,
without reserve,
and with boundless confidence,
for you are my Father.

It is not an easy prayer! It springs from the cross where the experience of having been abandoned preceded the decision to abandon oneself. One need only recall brother Charles's feelings on Christmas Day 1907 when he wrote in his notebook, "No Mass because I am alone." Many people have difficulty in saying this prayer. But it can become an interior compass, especially in the face of difficult situations: wars, personal anguish, interpersonal conflicts.

Abandoning himself would lead brother Charles on a journey that involved a lot of risks. He often spoke about having to "jump overboard." Having discerned that he needed to leave his hermitage in Nazareth to go and ask for priesthood, he wrote, "It's to jump overboard. . . . It means leaving the boat, like St. Peter, to walk on stormy seas."[220] He had to *jump overboard* when he left his be-

---

220. Notes at end of retreat at Ephrem, March 1898.

loved family to go to the Trappists, do the same when he left the Trappists to become a hermit in Nazareth, and do it again when he left Beni Abbès to begin an adventure with the Tuareg. Jumping overboard was never easy. He needed to get past a paralyzing fear. When writing to Msgr. Guérin to tell him that he had been invited to take part in a convoy touring Tuareg territory, he wrote, "Every change, every move fills me with dread, destabilizes and terrifies me. I fear making a wrong turn and being unable to cope."[221] Abandonment is not the easy confidence that comes in a moment of grace, but a leap into the dark, guided only by faith. Guy Coponet, who survived the deadly terrorist attack in the church of St. Etienne-du-Rouvray in July 2016, shared what the prayer meant to him as he lay in his own blood in front of the altar after having been stabbed three times:

> I prayed as I have never prayed in my life. I called upon all the saints I could think of. First of all, little brother Charles, also killed by a Muslim, in the desert. In my heart of hearts, I recited my favorite prayer: *"Father, I abandon myself into your hands; do with me what you will. . . . Into your hands I commend my soul."* I was in his hands. . . . I was convinced I was going to die, but I prayed. I contemplated my life and I was calm. I have never been so serene. Completely at peace. I had no remorse, only love in me. In fact, it was a moment of great bliss. Abandonment, total abandonment . . . like brother Charles and the Virgin Mary. I prayed to her like I had never prayed before. I knew that I was in good hands.[222]

---

221. Letter to Msgr. Guérin, June 30, 1903.
222. "Eyewitness report: Fr. Jacques Hamel's last moments," Aleteia, October 4, 2016, accessed online.

The word that gives abandonment its true spirit is *confidence*. The prayer of abandonment is first of all Jesus' prayer on the cross. In saying, *"My Father,* into your hands I commend my spirit," he gives his death meaning. Instead of being a victim, he becomes a subject who changes his death into a gift of himself to the One who directs his life. By calling him *Father* he chooses confidence. Encouraging the little sisters to this same attitude of confidence, little sister Magdeleine wrote: "Have you ever seen that often-repeated gesture of a young father pretending to toss his little child out over a cliff? And the child laughs and laughs because he knows well that no harm can ever come to him from his father."[223] The leap into the dark becomes a *need to give oneself out of love.*

Believing in the fruitfulness of your life

For brother Charles, abandonment changed an enduring perseverance which could have been tainted with self-will into love. Abandonment doesn't just express confidence in God, but also expresses confidence in God's work in us. Brother Charles had anticipated that when, still in Nazareth, he wrote:

> You tell me that I will be happy with that blessed happiness of the last day . . . that as miserable as I am, I am like a palm tree planted beside living waters . . . and that in due season I will bear fruit. . . . And you add: you will be a beautiful tree with leaves that are eternally green; and all your works

---

223. The Green Bulletin, internal document of the Little Sisters of Jesus, p. 40.

will prosper and bear fruit for all eternity. My God, how good you are.[224]

The fruit promised him doesn't just consist in the twenty or so congregations sprung from his spirituality, nor in the number of people who draw their inspiration from his life. The fruitfulness of the cross cannot be measured in numbers, because it consists in a birth to oneself that begets God in the world.

Birth demands letting go and it was in that kind of abandonment that he persevered. "With an infinite peace, I surrender my soul into His hands, and my little boat to His guidance and the breath of His Spirit."[225] That breath would sometimes blow a gale. During his night of discernment where he resolved to *jump overboard* by leaving Nazareth, he noted his feelings: "The absolute confidence that if I am faithful, God's Will will be done—not just despite the obstacles but thanks to the obstacles—obstacles being the sign that the thing is pleasing in the eyes of God—the weakness of human means is cause for strength—God uses crosswinds to lead us safely to harbor."[226]

In his Frigate[227] that sailed on a sea of sand in Tamanrasset, storms did come down and crosswinds did indeed blow. With time, perhaps he became much more of a sailor than a soldier, no longer fighting the waves but navigating their swell. As night fell on December 1, 1916, those waves steered him safe and sound into the hands of the Father.

---

224. Meditation on Psalm 1, Nazareth, 1897.
225. Letter to Marie de Bondy, March 28, 1903.
226. Notes at end of retreat in Ephrem, March 1898.
227. Nickname given by Laperrine to Charles's hermitage in Tamanrasset, which was about 49 feet long and 6 feet wide.

8

Epilogue

I have often wondered what brother Charles would think if he saw us, Little Brothers and Sisters of Jesus today. Would he recognize us as his own?

In 2015, at the community's invitation, I went to spend three months in Algeria, in those places where he himself had lived. His hermitage, the *Frigate*, is still there on the left bank of the wadi in Tamanrasset, but the sea of sand has been smothered in a layer of cement and asphalt. Camels have been replaced by four-wheel-drives and the brothers have had to build a fence around the Frigate to protect it from the trucks that grazed its walls as they parked all around. In 100 years Tamanrasset has gone from a population of 120 to 200,000. It includes a big slum full of sub-Saharan refugees on their way north.

Despite all the shouting and honking, I felt brother Charles's heartbeat in his hermitage, in a place where different worlds continue to clash with each other.

From there I went to Assekrem where he built his second hermitage. Up there you'd think that time had stopped. Ancient volcanoes spat up rock formations that create an extraordinary jagged landscape. Still today, "the view is more beautiful than anyone can express or even imagine."[228] I spent a month of prayer there. The only sounds were those of the wind and the wild donkeys. From time to time I could hear the cry of a *mula mula*, a little bird who is a bearer of glad tidings, according to the Tuareg.

---

228. Letter to Marie de Bondy, July 9, 1911.

There too, in that place where heaven and earth touch, I felt brother Charles's heartbeat.

At the end of the month, a little brother who lives year-round in Assekrem offered to accompany two other little sisters and me back down to Tamanrasset. It involved a trek of nearly forty miles through the desert. I dearly wished to go but I was slightly fearful. Our first outing, to go see Stone Age drawings three hours away, had revealed my weakness. I could tell that the brother was a bit worried about taking me. The evening before our trek I went into brother Charles's hermitage and begged him to help me. "Brother Charles, it's through books that I met you and now it's my only chance to know you through my feet. Help me to walk in this desert." He must have heard me because I felt an energy that surprised me.

The first day was magnificent. We camped halfway down near some *gueltas*, pockets in the granite that retain water after the rain.

We had been warned that the second day would be more arduous. We had to cross a huge granite plateau where black rocks seemed to have grown like cabbages. The heat increased as we descended. I couldn't think too much but just concentrated on putting one foot in front of the other. At the other edge of the plateau we had a drink, and looking at our bottles, we suddenly realized that we didn't have enough water. We had hardly enough for the meal and there was the rest of the journey. There was a moment of panic that could easily have given rise to mutual accusations. But we continued the road with a more serious step—together. During the final hours my tongue was stuck to my palate. I thought of the brother who was carrying most of our equipment, and the young sister whose ankle was giving her trouble. Once again, a prayer welled up from the bottom of my heart. "Brother Charles, we aren't of the same caliber as you, but we are your brothers and sisters. Help us." After half an hour the brother found a *guelta* in the bed of the wadi. Words cannot express what you feel when you find water in the desert.

During that climb down from Assekrem to Tamanrasset I discovered Charles as my brother. "*More admirable than imitable,*" they had said. Maybe . . . but I say that *he is not ashamed to call us his little brothers and sisters.*[229]

---

229. See Hebrews 2:11.

Selected Bibliography

Author's note: Rather than French texts that will be of little use to most readers, I have chosen to include existing references to Charles de Foucauld's life in English.

Bazin, René. *Charles de Foucauld: Hermit and Explorer.* London: Burns Oates and Washbourne, 1923.

Chatelard, Antoine. *Journey to Tamanrasset.* Bangalore: Claretian Publications, 2013.

Ellsberg, Robert. *Charles de Foucauld.* Maryknoll, NY: Orbis Books, 1999.

Lafon, Michel. *15 Days of Prayer with Charles de Foucauld.* Hyde Park, NY: New City Press, 2008.

Latham, Ian. *The Vision of the Gospel that filled the mind and heart of Brother Charles.* Kent: Oyster Press, 1993.

Little Sister Annie of Jesus. *Charles de Foucauld: In the Footsteps of Jesus de Nazareth.* London: New City, 2004.

Merad, Ali. *Christian Hermit in an Islamic World.* Mahwah, NJ: Paulist Press, 1999.

Six, Jean Francois. *Spiritual Autobiography of Charles de Foucauld.* Denville, NJ: Dimension Books, 1964.

Wright, Cathy, lsj. *Charles de Foucauld: Journey of the Spirit.* Boston: Pauline Books and Media, 2005.

New City Press

New City Press is one of more than 20 publishing houses sponsored by the Focolare, a movement founded by Chiara Lubich to help bring about the realization of Jesus' prayer: "That all may be one" (John 17:21). In view of that goal, New City Press publishes books and resources that enrich the lives of people and help all to strive toward the unity of the entire human family. We are a member of the Association of Catholic Publishers.

www.newcitypress.com
202 Comforter Blvd.
Hyde Park, New York

Periodicals
Living City Magazine
www.livingcitymagazine.com

Scan to join our mailing list
for discounts and promotions
or go to www.newcitypress.com
and click on "join our email list."